MAISIE STEVEN is a Highlander, brought up in Glenurquhart in Inverness-shire. As a nutritionist concerned with Scotland's food habits she wrote **The Good Scots Diet**, a review of diet and health from earliest times to the present. She was introduced to the Old Statistical Account by her late husband Campbell Steven, a prolific writer on outdoors Scotland. She fell under its spell, eventually producing **Parish Life in 18th Century Scotland**, which was shortlisted for the Longman History award. **The Heart is Highland**, her account of growing up in a Highland glen, has brought a warm response from readers far and wide who identify with its evocation of simplicity in family and community life. Maisie Steven lives in Aberfeldy in Perthshire. She is the mother of Dunkeld-based poet and writer Kenneth Steven.

Gems of Old Scotland

SCENES AND STORIES FROM
THE OLD STATISTICAL ACCOUNT
OF THE EIGHTEENTH CENTURY

Maisie Steven

illustrations by Scoular Anderson

ARGYLL✚PUBLISHING

First Published by
Argyll Publishing
Glendaruel
Argyll PA22 3AE
Scotland
www.argyllpublishing.com

The rights of the author have
been asserted by her in
accordance with the Copyright,
Designs and Patents Act 1988.

**British Library Cataloguing-in-
Publication Data.
A catalogue record for this book is
available from the British Library.**

ISBN 978 1 906134 12 9

Printing & Binding Bell & Bain Ltd,
Glasgow

For Ken and Ute
with love

CONTENTS

INTRODUCTION
The 18th Century Parish Accounts   7

1 Beginnings   11

2 Character   39

3 Lifestyle   53

4 Customs   75

5 Superstitions   87

6 Grievances   101

7 Initiatives   117

8 Outspoken Comments   139

9 Memorable Stories   159

APPENDIX I Some Interesting Statistics   179

APPENDIX II The questions   186

The Eighteenth Century Parish Accounts

I N THE YEAR 1790, an eminent Scotsman had the very ambitious idea of compiling a complete picture of the whole of Scotland.

His aim was altruistic. He hoped that a survey showing up both strengths and weaknesses would lead eventually to an improvement in the lot of the common people, many of whom were living on the edge of starvation. The main cause of their poverty was the abysmal state of agriculture at the time – and he was himself a keen agricultural improver.

He was Sir John Sinclair of Ulbster in Caithness, a Member of Parliament who had studied law at Edinburgh, Glasgow and Oxford and in addition, a rich landowner. He was therefore an ideal person to drive forward such an ambitious scheme. However, in view of the poor state of communications of the day, he was going to need a great deal of help.

He decided to call on the assistance of every parish minister in the country (all 938 of them) because not only were they a learned body of men, but they also knew the people and conditions within their parishes better than anyone else.

This immense undertaking began in May 1790 with Sir

John sending a circular letter to each minister. He could do this without charge because he was able to use the parliamentary frank. Along with this letter the unfortunate ministers received a list of 160 questions to which six others were later added.

A daunting questionnaire indeed!

It is not altogether surprising that many of the recipients took years to respond. Quite possibly they pushed it to the back of a drawer and tried to forget about it. In any case, it took Sir John nine whole years to extract the last of the reports. During this period he sent out numerous circular reminder letters, written in a persuasive but always gentlemanly tone but becoming more impatient as the years went on. The final one was written in red ink. All the same, it was he who had to apologise at one point for having lost twelve of the accounts. What dismay this must have caused in an age when everything was hand-written and possibly no copies had been kept.

It is only fair to add that those who took longest to reply were not necessarily lazy or negligent. On the contrary, some of the finest accounts arrived late following years of conscientious research. Many could easily have stood as books in their own right.

Needless to say, many majored on the aspects which most interested them, ignoring the other questions. Some come across as extremely well-informed, especially on the subject of agriculture. Only a few reports appear to have been scribbled hastily. On the whole they have been rated as anything from good to excellent.

What then was this fearsome list of questions all about? The short answer is – everything! There were questions about agriculture, industry, occupations, wages and prices. Questions about roads, bridges, canals, harbours, coasts, archaeology, geology, place-names, wildlife. Then there were questions about education, church life, beliefs, superstitions, food, housing, dress and fuel. Questions about family life, poor relief, health, diseases, games and amusements. There were even queries about unusual happenings like floods, storms and shipwrecks. As for the word 'statistical', it was a new word learned by Sir John from Germany at the time. It meant simply information, for example, lists of people in different age-groups, numbers of sheep and cattle, diseases and causes of death.

It would be difficult to think of any subject which was not of interest to Sir John (or indeed anyone today who may be following some special course of historical study). There was however an addendum to the daunting list which may have cheered some faint hearts.

> 'It is not expected that all the enclosed inquiries
> should be answered by any individual, nor is
> minute exactness called for.'

All the same, some of the most detailed and painstaking accounts do give the impression that the writers went out and counted every sheep.

In the end, what emerged is a fascinating picture of Scotland in that final decade of the eighteenth century – an era as it happens of maximum change, with agricultural advances, population movement, rising wages, improvements in housing and health (at least for the more fortunate), as well as the early stages of the Industrial Revolution. As is well-known, there was at the same time a great deal of intellectual activity which would later be known as The Enlightenment.

The Old Statistical Account, as the collected reports became known, has often been the envy of social historians elsewhere. Sadly, it has never been well-known in Scotland. Why is this? Has the word 'statistical' been off-putting? Certainly a very real obstacle in earlier times was that in his impatience, Sir John Sinclair published the reports higgledy-piggledy, just as they came in, meaning that one might find Dumfries, Dingwall and Dumbarton side by side.

It was not until the 1970s that the modern version was introduced. Historians Ian R Grant and Donald J Withrington organised the reports into twenty volumes with parishes grouped by county in alphabetical order.

This lack of recognition is a great pity, for these old accounts are brimful of human interest, offering fascinating insights into our ancestors' way of life. The writing in itself offers much of interest. It can be quaint and amusing, poignant, thought-provoking and at times flamboyant, and in many cases nothing short of brilliant.

Undoubtedly the Old Statistical Account is a great Scottish treasure. This is what has led me to write this book. It offers a selection of highlights which it is hoped will provide a flavour of the whole work.

'In this parish is a considerable nursery carried on by the Messrs Dickson.
It contains all kinds of fruit and forest trees, flower plants and roots,
and flowering shrubs, that are naturalised to this country'

CHAPTER I

Beginnings

ONE INTRIGUING aspect emerging from research into these old parish accounts has been early signs of issues that are still being debated today. Some prime examples might be the consequences of mass production, fishing rights, industrial pollution and who exactly are 'the deserving poor'. Times may have changed in radical ways, but some problems are clearly perennial!

At times, what seems like the sheer modernity may well cause surprise. Other situations illustrate just how little human nature changes even in two centuries. And while with twenty-first century arrogance it may be tempting to regard our modern ways as inevitably superior, we find here and there that our ancestors have something to teach us!

NURSERIES AND MARKET GARDENS

Finding thriving eighteenth century nurseries probably surprised me more than anything else, despite the fact that plant-hunting around the world was in full swing. Perhaps it was their advanced state which caused amazement – especially that of the Perth establishment. The account for Kinnoull, now part of the city, offers a full description. (XI, 294)

'About the year 1767, a nursery was begun in this parish,' wrote the minister.

'It contains between 30 and 40 acres of ground, on the east bank of the Tay, directly opposite Perth; for the cultivation of which the number of hands varies according to the exigencies of the season; but at an average, more than 40 find constant employment. The soil and exposure of these grounds are both remarkably fitted for rearing plants of such a vigorous and hardy nature, as are suitable not only to the sheltered, but to the exposed situations, with which the varied face of the country abounds.

'This nursery contains all kinds of fruit and forest trees, evergreen and flowering shrubs, flower roots and plants, which are naturalised to the climate. The proprietors have always been particularly careful in the selection of and proof of the various kinds of fruit-trees, and in consequence of this, the demand has always been very extensive. On the nursery grounds, they have lately erected a large extensive green-house, in which there is not only a numerous, but a rich collection of exotic plants. And at their shop in Perth, they keep a complete assortment of all kinds of garden, grass, tree and flower seeds.'

This remarkable eighteenth century nursery even had, so to speak, a mail order section.

> 'These various articles find a ready market not only in the rich adjacent country, but in the more remote parts of Scotland. They are frequently sent to England and Ireland.'

A few other reports from around the country offer some details of local nurseries, although not on a similar scale. One such comes from Hawick in the Borders: (III, 455)

> 'In this parish is a considerable nursery carried on by the Messrs Dickson. It contains all kinds of fruit and forest trees, flower plants and roots, and flowering shrubs, that are naturalised to this country; besides a great collection of exotic plants. At some seasons, there are 50 people employed in the nursery grounds.'

Some of the stately homes clearly had the means and expertise available for the production of exotica, as described for example in the report for Longforgan in Perthshire: (XI, 321)

> 'There are above 300 feet of glass; a melon-pit of 20ft by 12, nectarines, apricots, figs, almonds, and other fruits, which ripen on the open wall.'

The minister who wrote this report, clearly fascinated by the whole operation, proceeds to give a detailed (and to me totally baffling) description of the internal workings of the furnace.

MARKET GARDENING

In a few reports, generally from parishes near towns or cities, it is possible to identify the beginnings of market gardens, often supplying a single item for the urban population. One example comes from Prestonpans: (II, 577)

> 'Considerable quantities of cabbage plants are raised here. The season of sowing them is at Lammas. Besides the sale in the neighbourhood, 150,000 at a medium are sent annually to Glasgow, and about 70,000 to Falkirk and Carron. The severer the winter, the demand for them is greater.'

Considering the very few sources of Vitamin C available at the time, this must have been a valuable resource for the people, especially in winter.

And from Lasswade (II, 342) comes this comment:

> 'Gardening is carried on here to a considerable extent, and the attention of the gardeners is chiefly directed to the cultivation of strawberries, than which they have not a surer or more profitable crop. They depend less upon the season than other fruits; and when properly cultivated, this fruit will yield at an average, 18lbs from an acre. It may be observed, that it was in this parish that strawberries were first raised in any quantities for the public market.'

Finally, in the account for Banff (XVI, 22) there is mention of what sounds like an early allotment system:

> 'A few fields adjoining the town are rented as high
> as £5 and £6 the acre. These are chiefly occupied
> by gardeners, who raise pot herbs and other
> vegetables for the supply of the inhabitants.'

It would have been of interest to know what these were.

AN EARLY EXAMPLE OF OCCUPATIONAL THERAPY

The writer of the Montrose account (XIII, 542) describes a most remarkable 'lunatic asylum' in that town. Considering the paucity of hospitals of any kind in Scotland at the time – they are seldom mentioned outside of the main centres of population – to find something which does actually sound like some kind of department of occupational therapy is indeed astonishing. The sensitivity with which the 'lunatics', as they were then known, appear to have been treated in this establishment is altogether remarkable. How psychiatric patients must have fared in many other places scarcely bears thinking about.

'Several pieces of coarse sheeting have been made, from the yarn spun by the lunatics in their lucid intervals,' the minister tells us. 'At such times, they are also employed in painting, reading, gardening, knitting stockings, spinning and working a needle.' And lest it should be assumed that 'painting' referred merely to applying paint to walls, the writer adds, 'A piece of painting, in the mistress's room, done by one of the lunatics is, as such, a considerable curiosity.'

Could this department easily be bettered today?

FISHING RIGHTS

The issue of foreign fishers and the legality or otherwise of their catches is high on the agenda in twenty first century Scotland, especially on the east coast. It is therefore of undoubted interest to find in the account for Fraserburgh that this situation is far from new.

First the writer lists the species of fish normally caught there: (XV, 169)

> '. . . cod, ling, skate, turbot, whitings, haddocks,
> mackerel, lobsters and many other kinds of fish,
> all of the best quality, and often in great
> quantities, are caught in their seasons. The Dutch
> are in the practice of fishing in summer on this
> coast; and in 1786, came so near as to preclude
> the inhabitants from their usual stations. This
> practice has long been followed by them.'

In an age of poverty and hardship, long before any kind of social services, this must have caused much suffering to the people.

There is also, however, another side to the story of fishing in the Old Statistical Account. Rightly characterising some of his parishioners as courageous men, the writer of the account for Avoch in the Black Isle has this to say: (XVII, 316)

> 'In addition to the active enterprising spirit of
> these honest men, we may add, that three of the
> seatown crews having engaged in Spring 1791, to
> fish for several months on the coast of

> Northumberland, coasted it in their little open
> boats the whole way from Avoch to Beaduel,
> without either chart or compass, and returned in
> like manner, with no other accident, except
> splitting one of their sails.'

That this records a feat of seamanship is not in doubt. The only question is just what the Northumbrians thought of the presence of the Scots fishermen on their coasts.

CONSERVATION CONCERN

In just two of the parish accounts, I identified what would now be called conservation concern. The reports quoted below represent two different aspects of this concern.

The minister writing from Hutton and Corrie in the Borders (IV, 244) is incensed by the cruel practice of spearing spawning salmon, and writes with passion:

> 'Grilses and salmon and trout come far up in the
> spawning time. They do not meet with the same
> protection they do in most other waters in
> Scotland at that season. It is little wonder they
> should not, in the small waters of this parish,
> where the people are not benefited by them
> when the fish is of more value. But it is
> surprising, that even proprietors of fishings upon
> Annan kill salmon down to November, and see
> them destroyed under their eye with the LEISTER
> or spear, upon the spawn bed. The destruction of

> the ewe in lamb, or the hen upon eggs in March,
> would not more demonstrate the impolicy or
> depravity of man.'

It is on a different account that the writer of the report for Sorn, Dumfriesshire, voices his concern – industrialisation with its attendant pollution: (VI, 527)

> 'In the river of Ayr there was abundance of fresh-
> water trout, and some salmon; but it is here
> generally believed that they have of late been
> much diminished in their numbers by the iron
> and tan works of Muirkirk, and by the coal and
> lime works both in that parish and in the parish
> of Sorn.'

It need hardly be said that the situation was set to become altogether more serious and more widespread as the Industrial Revolution got under way.

AN EARLY LIBRARY

The account for Crawford in Lanarkshire (VII, 209) tells of a most unusual library – not to mention some highly unusual workers:

'Leadhills contain the most famous and ancient lead mines in Scotland,' claims the writer.

> 'There are nearly 200 men employed by the
> Scotch Mining Company. These are subdivided
> into pickmen, smelters, washers and labourers,

besides carpenters and smiths. They work in the
mines only six hours in the 24. Having therefore
a great deal of spare time, they employ
themselves in reading, and for this purpose have
been at the expense of fitting up a library, out of
which every one who contributes to the expense
receives books.'

FORESTRY

Out of a great many possible examples of enthusiastic
planters at the time of the Old Statistical Account, none is
more deserving of special mention than the Duke of Atholl
in Perthshire. Interestingly, Perthshire, widely known today
as Big Tree Country, has many famous and ancient trees still
flourishing.

The writer of the report for Little Dunkeld has much to
say on this subject: (XII, 402)

'Within 25 years past the Duke of Atholl has
planted 1000 acres in this parish. . . not only with
Scotch fir, but with a great proportion of larix
(larch); together with many thousands of oak,
ash, elm, plane, beech and other species; all
exceeding three millions of trees.'

From the neighbouring parish of Dunkeld (XII, 339-340)
comes a similar list of trees, but with several additions, and
an even greater planting record:

'. . . ash, beech, birch, larix, lime, oak, spruce,

lucombe oak, abel, Spanish chestnut, Scots elm,
Scots fir, New England fir, holly and thorn. The
Duke has planted upwards of 4000 acres.

'The planting of timber-trees, if the proper species
is chosen, is a profitable mode of cropping
ground, if not very valuable for the plough. It is
one which accumulates yearly in value, and will
fully repay, at the time of cutting it down, the
original cost, with interest for the sum, and rent
during the time of growth.'

Many of the writers, in the Borders especially, make an
eloquent plea for more planting to be carried out, citing the
advantages this would give in providing shelter for both
livestock and gardens.

Here and there it is clear that the principle of mixed planting is being followed, as for example in the report for Petty
on the Moray Firth: (XVII, 241)

'The Earl of Moray has, within the last twenty
years, inclosed and planted at least 500 acres of
what was till then bleak and barren heath. These
plantations consisted at first almost entirely of
Scots firs; but, as the firs grew up, they were
weeded and thinned to make room for trees of a
more valuable kind, chiefly oaks, which thrive
amazingly well, to which the firs serve as a
shelter.'

GERIATRIC CARE

These parish accounts offer many examples of what has been called 'the poor looking after the very poor'. However, they do not usually focus specifically on the elderly. It was the practice in certain areas, for example, for poor people to have bags left at the mills, into which 'everyone puts as much as he can spare, or as charity disposes him'.

Often too there was a tradition of going round collecting for those in need, as in Grange in Banffshire: (XVI, 227)

> 'On the Christmas holidays the young men go out
> in parties throughout the parish, a-begging for the
> greatest objects of charity; and several bolls of
> meal, and some pounds sterling of money, are
> collected every year, and committed to the care of
> members of session, for behoof of those for
> whom it is collected. This practice has an
> excellent effect upon the morals, both of young
> and old; it disposes the old to acts of liberality,
> and draws forth their sympathy towards the
> distressed; and it trains up the young to acts of
> benevolence and charity.'

In Assynt in Sutherland, though, a noteworthy scheme existed which was specifically designed for the care of the elderly – one which demonstrates clearly not only practical caring but also real sensitivity in seeking to preserve their dignity: (XVIII, 313)

> 'When anyone becomes old and feeble, their

nearest relations build a little comfortable house
for them, close to their own residence; and even
there the distaff and spindle is well managed.
These old matrons nurse the children of their
relations; the songs and airs of Fingal and ancient
heroes are sung in the Gaelic tongue, to which
the little children dance. Old men are prudently
engaged in some domestic affair, such as
repairing the houses of the neighbouring tenants
etc. In short, they share with their relatives all the
viands of the family.'

As a practical solution to a perennial problem, this could
scarcely be bettered, offering as it does preservation of the
culture, bonding between the generations, and occupational
therapy – not to mention a useful baby-sitting service!

AN EARLY TRADE UNION

The only example of the beginnings of Trade Unionism which
I found in the parish accounts come from Bonhill near
Dumbarton, at a centre of the cotton trade. It does not appear
to have fared well.

'They (the workers) appointed a committee of
their number, from the different printfields in the
West of Scotland, to meet to regulate the prices,
which they were to oblige their masters to give
for the different pieces of work. They were to

allow no persons to be employed, but such as came under certain regulations which they had framed. . . These measures obliged the masters to commence prosecutions, and to imprison some of their hands last summer, and a kind of compromise has been made between the masters and servants for a time; but it will be easily foreseen, that one of the parties must be in complete subjection to the other, before the trade can be upon a proper and sure footing.'

THE WEDDING INDUSTRY

I had read half-way through the account for Graitney when it dawned on me that this was the still-celebrated Gretna! And it was clear from the report that the writer, the 'regular and established clergyman' of the parish, was far from happy about the conduct of clandestine marriages as a flourishing local industry. No other explanation seems necessary, as the accounts speak adequately for themselves: (IV, 191)

'This parish has long been famous in the annals of matrimonial adventure, for the marriages of fugitive lovers from England, which have been celebrated here. People living at a distance erroneously suppose, that the regular and established clergyman of this parish is the celebrator of those marriages: whereas the persons who follow this illicit practice, are mere impostors, priests of their own erection, who have no right whatever, either to marry, or to exercise any part of the clerical function. There are, at present, more than one of this description in this place. But the greatest part of the trade is monopolised by a man who was originally a tobacconist, and not a blacksmith, as is generally believed. He is a fellow without literature and without principles, without morals, and without manners. His life is a continued scene of drunkenness.'

The following is a copy of one of the certificates of marriage, with the original spelling:

'THIS IS TO SARTSAY ALL PERSONS THAT MAY BE CONSERNID, THAT AB FROM THE PARISH OF C AND IN COUNTY D, AND EF FROM THE PARISH OF G AND IN THE COUNTY OF H, AND BOTH COMES BEFORE ME AND DECLAYRED THEMSELEFS TO BE SINGLE PERSONS, AND NOW MAYRIED BY THE FORME OF THE KIRK OF SCOTLAND, AND AGREIBLE TO THE CHURCH OF ENGLAND, AND GIVINE ONDRE MY HAND, THIS DAY . . . 1873'

The minister continues:

'Is it not a disgrace to the police of a civilized country, to permit irregularities to be practised with impunity? And is it not a reflection on the

good sense and discernment of the Nobility and
Gentry of England (for some of the English
Nobility have been married here), to suffer
themselves to be imposed upon, and their
pockets to be picked, by such miscreants?'

A CASUALTY OF INDUSTRIALISATION

These old parish accounts are full of surprises. It can happen
that, after rather idly wading through some tedious section
which covers familiar ground, one suddenly strikes gold! This
is how I recall coming upon the situation which was causing
concern to the writer of the Culross account. It followed a
long series of rural parishes in which, predictably, the
common occupations were weaving and agricultural
labouring: (XI, 106)

'There was formerly a species of manufacture in
some measure peculiar, if not altogether
confined, to this place, from 30 to 40 hands
having been usually engaged in it. This branch
was that of making girdles, a kitchen utensil well
known in Scotland for toasting unleavened bread.
By two royal grants, one of James IV and the
other Charles I, the girdlesmiths of Culross had
the sole and exclusive privilege of making girdles,
which were invented by them. But in the year
1727, the Court of Session found that no
monopolies of this kind could be granted, in

> prejudice of any royal burgh. The decline of the
> manufacture in Culross which has now dwindled
> almost to nothing, is, however, not so much to
> be ascribed to the loss of the patent as to the
> cheaper mode of making girdles by the Carron
> Company from the power of machinery.'

The loss of girdle-making must have been a severe blow to Culross, for up to this time the poorer folk of Scotland had depended largely on girdles for the making of oat bannocks, few having recourse to ovens. Except in a few more prosperous places, wheaten bread was used mainly by the rich. Now mass production had overtaken the trade. The Carron Ironworks, which had opened in Falkirk in 1759 is, incidentally, considered by many to represent the start of the Industrial Revolution in Scotland.

The girdle-makers may well have been the first casualty of this kind. Other trades, notably the home production of linen, were to follow. But this situation in Culross seems to set it on the world stage – loss of a valuable home-based industry has happened all over the world. It still happens today.

FRIENDLY SOCIETIES

In an age when many lived in poverty, it is of particular interest to find in the institution of Friendly Societies a courageous attempt to help poor people, as far as they were able, by making provision for times of special hardship.

Interestingly, all the examples I have found in the accounts come from either Ayrshire or the Borders; in only two of these is there any description given of how exactly they were administered. (IV, 374)

> 'A Friendly Society was instituted in Langholm following a season of scarcity, which has been productive of beneficial consequences. There are 150 members, who pay a shilling quarterly. A member will be expelled for habitual drunkenness, insolence to any of the office-bearers, or gross immorality.'

Members unable to work were to receive 4s6d per week 'on attestation of surgeon' (an early example of today's sick note?) and, if the illness was prolonged for more than a year and a half, 2s per week for life. When a member died, all the others were to attend the funeral.

Pitifully small as the 'pensions' may seem to us today, one can easily imagine what those sums must have meant to hard-pressed folk when, for example, the family breadwinner suffered some injury or debilitating disease.

The account for Galston in Ayrshire illustrates a somewhat different working method: (VI, 226)

> 'One such society is established in this parish. It consists of about 50 members, and is called the penny or halfpenny society. It has no funds, which are too apt to be embezzled; but, when a brother is confined to bed by sickness, every

member pays him a penny weekly, and if he is
able to go about, if not to work, a half-penny.
This institution is found to answer; and might be
adapted in other places with advantage.'

A third and notably sensitive description comes from
the report from Kirkpatrick-Durham: (V, 245)

'A few months ago, a society of a charitable
complexion was established in the parish.
Societies of this description are becoming
frequent in this part of the country, and they
seem to deserve encouragement, because the
delicacy of the human feelings will be less hurt,
when supplies are received from a source of this
kind, than from the ordinary sources of charity.'

It is noteworthy that this element of sturdy independence
and general abhorrence of anything that smacks of charity is
very often encountered throughout the Old Statistical
Account.

PLANS FOR CANALS

Today, the Caledonian Canal which cuts through northern
Scotland is a familiar feature and of undoubted usefulness
to sailors. Back in the 1790s it was only an idea – and an
ambitious one for the time. Mention of such a possibility in
the account for Inverness is of interest here. Indeed there
seems to be no limit to this writer's vision! (XVII, 106)

'A navigable canal, from the west sea at Fort
William, to the east sea at Inverness, would no
doubt be beneficial to the country at large, but
more immediately to a very extensive tract of the
Highlands, which is now covered with sheep, and
almost depopulated. Woollen manufactures
would soon be established, other manufactures
follow of course, villages and the cheerful haunts
of men insensibly arise, and population in a few
years increase amazingly in a district which, alas!
at present, is dreary to the traveller, filling him
with melancholy and dejection of heart.'

This Inverness writer's hopes are echoed, with slightly
less passion, by the writer of the account for Kilmallie near
Fort William: (XVII, 150)

'The improvement which would be of the greatest
advantage to the parish, and indeed to the whole
kingdom, would be to cut a canal between the
west and the east seas. . . It could easily be
accomplished.'

Some thirty years later, with the opening of the canal
built by Thomas Telford, the vision was fulfilled.

AGRICULTURAL IMPROVEMENTS

Until around the middle of the eighteenth century, agriculture
in Scotland had been in an abysmal state, with much of the
land undrained, unfertilised and choked with weeds. There

was little understanding of crop rotation, implements were antiquated and the livestock was woefully malnourished.

Now, however, the movement towards improvement was on in earnest, albeit in a completely piecemeal fashion around the country. Out of a great many possible examples, a few will serve to highlight the work of the 'improvers'. These were principally landowners and wealthy farmers who set new trends and convinced many doubters of the pressing need for change.

One of these is described by the writer of the report from Sorn in Ayrshire: (VI,549)

> 'The first person who carried out rural improvement to any considerable extent in this parish was the late Countess-dowager of Loudon . . . At that time (1727) the parish was in a very uncultivated state, and the whole aspect of the country dreary and uncomfortable. In a soil and climate where roads and shelter were peculiarly necessary, not a single road or hedge, and very few trees, were to be seen. Not discouraged by these unfavourable circumstances, she determined to create a scene more congenial to her own taste, and more like the scenes to which she had been accustomed in a better country. Accordingly, her skill and activity gradually produced an agreeable change. Besides enlarging and improving the garden and orchard, she subdivided an extensive farm which she

occupied herself, enclosed it with hedges and
hedgerows, and interspersed it with belts and
clumps of planting. . . These operations she
herself carefully superintended, and many both of
the fruit and forest trees were actually planted
and pruned by her own hands.'

It has to be said that in many of the descriptions of
outstanding improvements, credit is freely given (as above)
to the example offered by agricultural practice south of the
border. One such comes from the account for Athelstaneford
in East Lothian: (II, 452)

'It would be improper not to mention in a
publication of this kind the following character.
His name is John Walker. He was the first farmer
in this country who ever fallowed an acre of land,
or sowed a boll of wheat on what was commonly
called outfield land. He took the hint from an
English gentleman travelling in the country. When
he began the experiment, many of his neighbours
laughed at his seeming folly, while his more
immediate connections were alarmed at the
circumstance of his not sowing his fields, and
considered it a symptom of poverty. His crop
exceeded his most sanguine expectations, and
justified the wisdom of his conduct; and his
neighbours had the good sense to follow his
example.'

Many of the accounts include eulogies of outstanding pioneers in agriculture. A final example will suffice. It comes from the parish of Ecclesgrieg or St Cyrus in Kincardineshire: (XIV, 94)

'The lands might have remained in their original state, had not the late Robert Scott, Esq., of Dunninauld, been induced, from the lime rocks within the flood mark at Milton, to rent the farm bearing that name. As he was representative in Parliament for the county of Forfar, in going up and coming down from London, he was not inattentive to the system of agriculture followed in England. Finding it superior to any hitherto practised in Scotland, he tried to follow it, first upon his own estate, and afterwards upon the farm of Milton. He set the example of draining, stoning, liming, fallowing, cleaning, manuring, and properly dressing the fields on this farm. The consequence was, he raised great crops of all sorts of grain, as well as of grass. The farmers, who at first held his plan in derision, and were unwilling to leave their own old beaten track, began to be surprised at his great crops; and when experience demonstrated to them the success of his schemes, they gradually turned round to imitate them. Hence arose a spirit of agriculture, and even of emulation of it, which has produced the happiest effects.'

EDUCATION

About a century before the Old Statistical Account was written, in the reign of William and Mary, an Act had been passed with the aim of ensuring that each parish should have a school and schoolmaster, the maximum salary to be 300 merks Scotch and the minimum 200. At the time, these rates were acceptable; now, following on a period of inflation, they were totally inadequate, forcing most of the country's valuable and highly-educated dominies to live in what one writer called 'a genteel kind of starving'.

Not surprisingly, then, in many reports the ministers speak out strongly against the exploitation of the schoolmasters – with some bravery, it should be added, since they risked causing grave offence to the landed gentry ('heritors') who were also their own employers.

Here and there, however, there are to be found interesting snippets which shed light on some of the ways educational problems were being solved, and – who knows? – these may even have something to teach us in the twenty first century. The account for Dunoon reads: (VIII, 92)

> 'Winter Schools are taught by children from 12-15
> years of age, who go from house to house, for
> about 20s. and their maintenance, to teach younger
> children than themselves; and it is surprising with
> what success they go about that business.'

Winter schools were at the time fairly common, since many children were employed in summer herding cattle.

In the account for Bothwell in Lanarkshire we find the

beginnings of an emphasis on practical skills, something which is still an issue today:

> 'This country is employed in agriculture, manufactures and commerce. . . The bulk of mankind have neither the time or money to procure a liberal education; a scheme of this kind brings instruction within their reach, and tends to reconcile them to it; would produce genius and improvements in mechanics, manufactures, in all professions; and communicates to the generality of the people various branches of knowledge of which they are at present destitute.'

Here and there are to be found the beginnings of specialised teaching skills, as in the case of a remarkable teacher in Duplin and Aberdalgy, Perthshire, of whom the minister writes with great respect: (XI, 162)

> 'It will not be deemed improper to add that he has acquired without any instructor, the rare talent of communicating knowledge to the deaf and dumb, and of teaching them to speak.'

The beginnings of night schools are also to be observed, as from this report from Campsie, Stirlingshire: (IX, 261)

> 'There being several works in the parish, the night school is considerable, being wholly taken up with grown persons, who attend for the purposes of writing, arithmetic etc.'

The use of older children in imparting knowledge to younger ones has already been noted; other forms of supplementary teaching are also of interest. One is the employment of disabled people. The nature of their disability is not given. In Eckford in the Borders the writer explains:

> 'As the school is not centrical, some infirm
> persons are employed to teach young children at
> a distance the English language, and the
> elementary principles of religion from the
> catechism. They are furnished with a house
> gratis, from the farmers, and satisfied with what
> the parents can afford.'

A final example of the solution to the problem of scarce and distant schools is one which would surely pose a challenge in today's more materialistic climate. . . the use of voluntary teachers! The account for Kirkmichael in Perthshire has this:

> 'At particular times of the year, especially in
> winter, some persons voluntarily assume the
> office of schoolmasters in the remoter parts of
> the parish and teach reading of English and
> writing.'

A CASE OF FEMALE EMANCIPATION

When looking at the life of the ordinary folk of eighteenth century Scotland, one certainly does not expect to find a great deal about the role of women. For the most part, they are to be found toiling hard behind the scenes, working day and night to bring up their children and put food on the table. This description of the wives of fishermen in Nigg, Kincardineshire, for example, seems to sum up all too accurately the kind of life they led:

> 'The woman, who has been from 3 or 4 o'clock (in the morning) carrying home fuel, or engaged at the rocks, bears the fish to market, 5 miles distant to some, and comes back to household affairs. . . During some later months of winter, the subsistence of the family has depended much on the work of the females. . . The whole female part of the parish, when not occupied by these engagements, or harvest, the moss (peats) and domestic affairs, work at knitting woollen stockings.'

And in the account for the east coast parish of Rathven: (XVI, 393)

> 'The fisher-wives lead a most laborious life. They assist in dragging the boats on to the beach, and in launching them. They sometimes, in frosty weather, and at unseasonable hours, carry their husbands on board, and ashore again, to keep them dry.'

The picture being one of unremitting toil and probable servility, it is all the more remarkable to find in Inveresk near Edinburgh a very different class of fisherwomen – remarkable in that they had somehow attained a state of independence which might well have been unique at the time: (II, 295)

> 'Four days a week they carry fish in creels to Edinburgh (a journey of 5 miles); those who carry fish gain at least 1s per day.' (This was roughly the wage of a skilled artisan at the time.)

> 'From the kind of life these women lead, it may naturally be concluded that their manners are peculiar, as they certainly are. Having so great a share in the maintenance of the family they have no small share in it, as may be inferred from a saying not unusual among them. When speaking of a young woman reported to be on the point of marriage, 'Hout!' they say, 'how can she keep a man, who can scarce maintain hersel?' As they do the work of men, their manners are masculine, and their strength and activity equal to their work.'

One thing can be said of these old parish accounts – they are full of surprises!

'The people in general are sober, industrious and humane.
The number of poor they support shows their humanity'

CHAPTER 2

Character

FEW ASPECTS of the Old Statistical Account can be more intriguing than the question of the character of our forebears. What were they really like? Considering for example that in material terms they were mostly very poor, were they more generous, or more greedy, than ourselves? How did the Scots' reputation for meanness arise, and was it fair? Were they honest? How did they treat those in need? Were they hardworking, or lazy? And did they have any outstanding faults, or on the other hand are there perhaps some lessons we could learn from them today?

Of course, at a distance of more than two hundred years, it isn't really possible to give assured answers to such questions; nor are generalisations ever satisfactory. In addition, this particular 'history' is filtered through the views, often strongly expressed, of the 938 ministers who penned the reports, making it at best highly subjective. When it is a question of facts – if you like, 'statistics' – how many horses or cattle in a parish; how many persons over 70; which diseases are most prevalent – we can be reasonably sure of accuracy. But when we find one minister praising his flock unreservedly, while his colleague in a neighbouring parish seems to take an altogether harsher view, we tend to find ourselves looking not so much at the people's character as at that of the minister concerned! Was the first one merely tolerant or the second a shade cantankerous? We shall never know!

It has to be said that some of the writers appear to be struggling to answer with complete impartiality. The minister of Kingussie in Inverness-shire has this to say: (XVI, 202)

> 'Like most of the inhabitants of the Highlands, they are brave, hospitable and polite. Their vices may be said to be grafted to their virtues. They are quarrelsome, addicted to drunkenness, and little to be depended on for the sincerity of their profession.'

This sounds an honest appraisal and certainly not unduly flattering. This writer, however, shows much humanity in his criticism, taking pains in an addendum to underline the miserable poverty in which his people live:

> 'Should a people thus obnoxious to poverty, and all its train of concomitant evils, be found less scrupulous in some particular than others who enjoy a happier lot; perhaps the liberal mind would find some alleviation of their errors in the necessity of their situation.'

Another writer striving for total honesty is the minister of Kinloch in Perthshire: (XII, 618)

> 'On the whole, the people are benevolent, humane, and charitable; but if we keep in view the great standard of perfection which the divine

Author hath left for our imitation, I must say that,
upon a close examination, there are to be seen
on the face of this fair character, some specks.'

One characteristic on which most seem to be agreed is
the honesty of the ordinary folk. Here again a ouple of reports
are noteworthy. One, from the Isle of Mull (Kilfinichen and
Kilviceuen) tells a remarkable story (which would arguably
be even more remarkable today!): (XX, 320)

'The people in general are sober, industrious and
humane. The number of poor they support
shows their humanity, as also two shipwrecks
that happened within these six years. In both
instances, the poor sailors were treated with
kindness and humanity. One of these vessels was
wrecked in Ross; and it is remarkable, that a
quantity of cork, very useful and much wanted
for their nets, scattered over a strand of upwards
of a mile in extent, was not touched by the
inhabitants, though many were too poor to buy it,
even if they had the opportunity.'

Another anecdote, again connected with the sea, is also
used to illustrate the people's kindness. This time it comes
from the east coast, the parish of Banchory Davinick in
Kincardineshire: (XIV, 14)

'On the 19th of August 1710, seven boys about
15 years of age each, sailed out of the harbour of
St Andrews in a little boat, and losing one of their

oars, were driven into the ocean. After six days and six nights of continual fasting and labour, they got to shore alive four miles south of Aberdeen, and 50 north of St Andrews. A humane country man, John Shepherd, kindly received them into his house, and sent information of so moving an accident to the magistrates of Aberdeen, who despatched their dean of guild, a physician, and a surgeon to attend them. All the boys were preserved in life, except the two youngest, who died soon after they came ashore. John Shepherd was presented with a silver cup by the father of one of the boys, in testimony of his gratitude for the active part he took in recovering his son.'

While this records merely a single instance of kindness, many reports tell of more general caring on the part of the poor people (historians have characterised the ethos of the day as 'the poor looking after the very poor') as is illustrated in the following account from Clatt in Aberdeenshire: (XV, 62)

'Such poor as live in or about the most populous villages are supplied, by their beneficent neighbours, with some little necessaries which they could not otherwise procure, such as milk, whey, turnips, potatoes, fuel etc. . . When it is known that any old or infirm person is in want, it is customary for the young lads to go out in an

evening though the parish, and to ask for meal,
or a little money, which the people very
cheerfully give; and it proved a most seasonable
supply to several who would be in hazard of
suffering want.'

It seems especially noteworthy that it is 'young lads'
who carry out this compassionate work; in another report,
that for Dunkeld in Perthshire, it is a woman: (XII, 333)

'Janet Macgregor was maidservant to a
respectable family. The parents died and the
children, then in infancy, were very destitute. The
poor woman clung to them with a parent's
affection, and in supporting and rearing the
orphans, spent the hard-won earnings of a
number of years.'

A balanced view must be maintained, however – the
people were not altogether saintly! While, as has been noted,
their honesty was stressed again and again, it has to be
remembered that the ministers were well aware that their
assessments would one day become public; it would thus
be difficult for them to highlight dishonest acts. One such,
all the same, is quoted in the following amusing excerpt
from the account for Gargunnock in Stirlingshire: (IX 365)

'Two old women, sisters, had for many years
every appearance of extreme indigence, though
without making application for assistance from
the parish. One of them at last applied to be

received on the poor's list, and, as no doubt was entertained of her poverty, she received 4s. per month. She died about six months after commencement of her pension. On examining the bedclothes, one purse of gold and silver was found after another, till the sum amounted to upwards of £40 sterling. Some old chests and barrels were found stored with beef, meal, cheese and various other provisions; and it was evident that the poor woman had lived in great affluence. The relations of the deceased, on hearing of the discovery, came from a distance to lay claim to her effects. But according to the settled rule of the parish, she had bequeathed all her effects to the poor, at the time she was received on to the poor's list. One half was allowed to be the property of her sister, who had received no pension from the parish. The other half became the property of the Kirk Session, to the great mortification of the relations; who certainly deserved this disappointment, as they had taken no notice of the deceased while she lived.'

By no means all of the ministers showered their parish-ioners with compliments. A fairly common complaint, for example (especially perhaps in the north of Scotland) was that the people were idle, as for instance in this report from Halkirk in Caithness: (XVIII, 81)

'We have rather too many who are idly disposed,

and who will not work, unless compelled to it by the extremity of the last necessity; for if they happen to have what will enable them to hold out until night, or any prospect of any other shift, though at the expense of their more industrious neighbours, to whom they are no small burden, they have no concern about their debts, or any provision for tomorrow. Though these are a grievance to the country, yet the British army is much indebted to them; and indeed, if this is a relief to themselves, it is no small one to their neighbours, who are glad to be rid of such useless drones.'

No less outspoken is another minister, again from a Caithness parish; in a caustic comment he brands his people as not only lazy but nosey as well! (XVIII, 24)

'During their hours of idleness, which are many, languor and lassitude are ever observable about them. The mind, having no interests of its own to fasten upon, exerts its power, for the sake of employment, in making investigations into the condition and character of others. Hence that solicitude after news, that spirit of prying into the most hidden concerns of their neighbours, with the view of gratifying curiosity rather than malevolence. Their discernment of the purposes of others, and dexterity in concealing their own, are no less remarkable.'

From time to time under the heading of character, a somewhat unlikely topic will be brought in. In the report for Kilberry and Kilcalmonnell in Argyll, for example, the people's affection for dogs is clearly a source of annoyance for the writer – not without justification in view of the overall poverty of the time. (VIII, 186)

> 'The most unaccountable part of the conduct of the lower classes in this and other parishes, and that which can be least easily reconciled to the hardships of their situation, is their fondness for dogs. Almost every family has one; and in some families there are two or three. Even paupers were found to have so unwarrantable an attachment to these animals, that threats to strike them off the poor's roll were obliged to be used before they could be prevailed upon to part with them. From the statistical table, it appears there are 400 dogs in the parish. The food devoured by these animals would feed 400 pigs, which, when a year old, would sell at £400.'

(It does indeed seem remarkable that some families should have found the means to keep two or three dogs alive; less surprising, perhaps, that a wandering beggar might have felt the need to keep a dog for protection.)

In contrast to the above, the well-known Scots characteristic of thrift is highlighted. In an entry in the account for Dalmeny, Lothians, we read: (II, 729)

> 'In Scotland, many half-starve themselves in
> order to make savings; not a few by several
> pounds sterling, which they reserve for old age,
> for putting their children to apprenticeships, or for
> otherwise bettering their own condition or that of
> their families.'

This writer then proceeds to add a glittering list of what he considers outstanding Scottish achievements:

> 'A spirit for enterprise and for rising in the world
> characterises the Scots in general; and this has so
> remarkably pervaded all ranks for these 40 or 50
> years past, that perhaps no people have in so
> short a period made so great advances in
> industry, agriculture, manufactures, refinement,
> and public wealth, as the people of Scotland!'

A sense of balance is surely required! And indeed a somewhat different assessment of the Scottish character comes across in the answer which numerous writers give to Sir John's question on drinking habits. (As to the general accessibility of alcohol, it is revealing to note, for example, that the town of Dunbar, with a population of only 3,700, boasts 46 licensed public houses). From Langholm in the Borders comes this comment: (IV, 366)

> 'The most contagious pestilence that ever
> desolated a country cannot produce more
> dreadful effects upon the natural than it is now
> producing in the moral world, upon every public

and private virtue. . . Licentiousness, under the
sacred (though prostituted) name of liberty, fraud,
robbery, murder, insanity, and suicide,
everywhere mark its fatal progress.'

This wholesale condemnation is shared by others from
the Borders; from the north various ministerial voices also
join in wholehearted opposition to the all-too-cheap and
easily available whisky. This excerpt from Kiltearn in east
Ross-shire is typical of many: (XVII, 493)

'These whisky-houses are much frequented by
tipplers and dram-drinkers, who sometimes sit
up whole nights at their debauch. Such tippling-
houses have provided a great nuisance for
several years past, and have been very prejudicial
to the health, the morals, and the circumstances
of several inhabitants of the parish. It is not
uncommon to see two mechanics [tradesmen] or
day labourers, repairing once or twice a-day to
one of these ensnaring haunts, and drinking a
choppin bottle of unmixed whisky each time.'

The writer, clearly concerned over the consequences for
these men's families, adds:

'What greatly adds to the grievance is, that the
keepers of these corrupting haunts are not always
scrupulous as to the mode of receiving payment
for this drink. When money fails, they will receive
meal and victual at a low price, which is often

stolen from the mills, and farmers' barns. When
this resource fails, they will even receive
household furniture and wearing apparel.'

This concern for vulnerable families clearly motivates
many of the condemnatory comments of the parish
ministers, some of whom mention with regret the passing
of the habit of drinking 'good, wholesome home-brewed
ale'. This had virtually come to an end because the Malt Tax,
brought in in 1725 (6d on every bushel of malt) had so
increased the price of 'twopenny ale' that whisky-drinking
had displaced it.

It is altogether typical of the Old Statistical Account,
however, that no generalisations can ever be made; a
divergent view is always to be found somewhere! In a few
parishes, then, it would appear that whisky-drinking had
actually declined – as described in the following report from
Traquair in the Borders: (III, 909)

'Within less than 30 years, the people of this
parish have changed their character very much
for the better. They were then much addicted to
drinking to excess. There were at that time more
than six alehouses; at present there is only one
publichouse, which is seldom if at all frequented
but by those who are transacting business, or by
travellers, and is on these accounts necessary.'

This decline would appear to be borne out by this amusing observation from the writer of the Banff account: (XVI, 60)

'1748: A joyous company, after dinner, have been
seen quaffing the wine of a dozen bottles from a
single glass.
1798: A sober party sometimes meet, whose libation
consists of a solitary bottle, with a dozen glasses.'

While the ministers' wholesale condemnation of excessive dram-drinking comes as no surprise, their antagonistic
attitude towards the use of tea certainly does. One after
another speaks out against its supposedly harmful effects –
perhaps none with such flamboyance as the minister for
Crieff: (XII, 290)

'Above 20 times more tea is used now than 20 years
ago', he writes.

'Bewitched by the mollifying influence of an
enfeebling potion, the very poorest classes begin
to regard it as one of the necessities of life, and
for its sake resign the cheaper and more
invigorating nourishment [milk, or ale?] which
the productions of their country afford.'

Interestingly, the writer from the parish of Eday and
Stronsay in Orkney offers the cheapest intoxicating liquor of
the entire 938 reports! (XIX, 325)

'A mineral spring is to be found among the rocks
on the east coast of the island of Stronsay. The
water, clear as crystal, not unpleasant, is full of
fixed air, as may be easily discovered by any who
drink some glasses of it; for they will soon find

> themselves affected in the same way, as if they
> had drunk some fine brisk bottled small beer.'

On reflection, one can see that of all of Sir John's questions, this one on character was probably the one which caused most heart-searching. Two final excerpts may suffice to illustrate the writers' dilemma.

The account for Mortlach in Angus appraises the situation frankly: (XVI, 334)

> 'It here obviously occurs, that a minister may be
> induced from various motives, to go to the extreme of
> truth, on the favourable side for his flock. His regard
> for them may blind and mislead him; or by condemn-
> ing them, he may think that he obliquely condemns
> himself; at least, if another did it, he might perhaps be
> led too readily to think so. Few chuse to depreciate
> their own importance; few to diminish the happy
> effects of their pastoral care; and fewer still are
> inclined to render themselves ungracious. Thus it may
> often place a clergyman in a delicate situation to be
> obliged to characterise his parishioners.'

As for the minister from the parish of Kilsyth, his particular 'delicate situation' was certainly not in doubt! 'the characters of the inhabitants of this parish are as varied as their counten-ances', is his careful comment. 'As in every mixed society, the good and the bad are blended together'. And then, reveal-ingly, he adds: 'Upwards of 500 of them are my blood relations.' (IX, 508)

'For men, the wearing of a hat (replacing the traditional blue bonnet) seems to have been considered a sure sign of affluence and respectability'

CHAPTER 3
Lifestyle

FROM THE PERSPECTIVE of our relatively affluent lifestyle today, it is difficult if not impossible to visualise the sheer harshness of the conditions faced by the vast majority of poorer folk in Scotland two hundred years ago. Yet the old parish accounts, while telling little of the lives of the gentry and richer people, do offer an intimate first-hand picture of ordinary living which at least aids our imagination.

It would seem helpful to begin by looking at what the Old Statistical Account has to say about the prized possessions – 'designer goods' – of the day. One might have expected these to be cattle or other livestock, as is the case in many primitive societies. Not so, as it appears from these accounts; rather it is certain special items, of which the most commonly-mentioned are clocks and watches, hand-bellows, spinning-wheels and especially tea-kettles. Not surprisingly, various articles of dress were also highly valued, particularly by the women – and the fancier the better! As for the men, above all the wearing of a hat (replacing the traditional blue bonnet) seems to have been considered a sure sign of affluence and respectability.

Following the disastrous Jacobite Rising of 1745, large numbers, especially in the Highlands, had been left in an abysmal state and often on the edge of starvation. Some fifty years later, a slow but significant improvement had taken place, although (as is everywhere true of the Old Statistical Account) with much variation and even at times between adjacent parishes. Interestingly, many reports begin by looking back, to demonstrate beneficial changes.

One such is from the parish of Lethnot in Angus: (XIII, 387)

> 'Within these last fifty years, a great alteration has taken place in the manners, dress, and way of living of the people in this place. Then, there was neither a spinning-wheel nor a reel within the parishes, except the minister's; now there is not a farm-house without one, and several of the sub-tenants use this same piece of furniture.'

Generally speaking, cottars lived at a much lower level than farmers. Once again, however, an interesting exception to this rule is to be found, in this comment from the Northern Isles which describes an unusually egalitarian society – Rousay and Eglishay: (XIX, 199)

> 'There is no difference in manners and habits between the cottager and the master of the farm. The master often turns to cottager, and the cottager sometimes becomes the master. They all take social snuff together. Their houses and their furniture are exactly the same.'

A fascinating glimpse from earlier times comes from the

parish of Benholme in Kincardineshire: (XIV, 50)

> 'About fifty years ago, the Excise Officer's family
> was the only one in Johnshaven that made use of
> tea; when the tea-kettle was carried to the well, to
> bring in water, numbers both of children and
> grown people followed it, expressing their
> wonder, and supposing it to be 'a beast with a
> horn'. In those days of simplicity, a watch or an
> 8-day clock would have created equal surprise.
> Now the tea-kettle has lost the power of
> astonishing, having become a necessary piece of
> furniture among the meanest.'

Looking next at improvement in dress, we find a fairly regular pattern, standards have improved greatly over the past few decades. But it is in answering Sir John Sinclair's question: 'Are the people economical, or expensive and luxurious for their circumstances?' that the ministers really let themselves go. Many of them are clearly incensed at what they see as an 'excessive love of luxury' even if in some cases this turns out to mean merely the wearing of a silk cloak, or simply a few ribbons, to church. To be fair, this is not true of all, and in some accounts there is gratitude for the fact that poor folk are not quite as poor as they were.

From a great many comments, one or two of the most outspoken will serve as illustration. The attitude of many writers is the same: the people should know their place and stick to it. However, in their defence it should be added that they were also genuinely concerned for the people's welfare, and aware that excessive expenditure on dress might well endanger the all-too-scarce resources of a family. This was especially relevant, it seems, in the case of young women being married. One writer asserts that 'they enter into marriage with their whole substance on their back'. And the minister from Dunoon is clearly in agreement: (VIII, 93)

> 'The young woman, who fifty years ago thought
> of endeavouring to make 100 or 200 merks for
> her portion, now sinks all the money she makes,
> in dress and ornament.'

Other writers are concerned over expenditure on clothes of 'foreign' manufacture to the neglect of their own productions. One even suggests offering a prize for 'the man who had the best suit of clothes spun in his house, and to the woman who had the best plaid, gown and petticoat of her own spinning'. There was also a clear concern about health, particularly in view of the miserably cold and damp dwellings which were the norm. The writer from Kirkconnel asserts: (IV, 273)

> 'It would seem not unnatural to suppose that to
> the modern passion for this light, flimsy, airy
> dress, so prevalent among all ranks, so
> unsuitable to the constitutions of all, may be
> ascribed no small share of the equally common
> prevalence of colds, fevers, rheumatisms,
> asthmas and consumptions.'

One minister makes a passionate plea for his special

panacea – the wearing of flannel at all times!

Although most of the blame fell on the women, the men were not exempt. They too must remember to keep their proper place. In another comment in which he compares new with old, the Montquhitter minister in Aberdeenshire writes: (XIV, 545)

> 'Nowadays, hats, broad cloth, good linen
> adorned with ruffles, are occasionally worn by all
> ranks of men. And the gentry can only be
> distinguished from plebeians by their superior
> manner, and by that elegant simplicity in dress
> which they now admire.'

Later, he continues:

> 'Formerly the blue bonnet adorned every head.
> Whenever a hat appeared, an idea of opulence,
> literature or rank immediately excited profound
> obeisance.'

This sentiment is echoed in many of the reports, along with, at times, a sense of genuine regret for the passing of the traditional blue bonnet. Perhaps, though, the most revealing statement comes from Kildrummy, also in Aberdeenshire, highlighting the sartorial improvements which had taken place: (XIV, 545)

> 'The dress of apprentice boys, at church and
> market, is superior to the finery of the young
> nobility of ancient times.'

Housing also serves as a kind of barometer of the lifestyle of the day. The picture on the whole is bleak, with some ministers asserting their belief that some dwellings are more fitted for livestock than human beings. One example comes from Clunie in Perthshire: (XII, 266)

> 'The materials for building houses abound in the parish, yet many of the people live in miserable smoky cribs, more like sties for hogs than habitations for men.'

From a different part of the country (Libberton in Lanark-shire), the writer agrees: (VII, 502)

> 'The best way to meliorate the people's condition is to give them better houses; for at present, the cottages and many of the farm houses are fitter for the habitations of beasts, than of human beings.'

Elsewhere the houses are referred to as 'mean, dirty hovels', 'shabby, smoky huts', 'wretched, damp dwellings'. Small wonder then that 'the rheumatism and sundry fevers' are cited over and over again as the predominant ailments of the people.

Here and there around the country, housing improve-ments were on the way, planned villages were beginning to be built and 'ideal homes' emerging, with such enviable features as slated roofs, gardens, and most desirable of all – windows with glass. In Kirkpatrick-Juxta, clearly a favoured area, the minister writes: (IV, 348)

> '70 years ago there was not a pane of glass,
> except in two houses – now every house has at
> least one glass window.'

The report for Little Dunkeld tells of: (XII, 423)

> 'landlords beginning to collect weavers and other
> handycraftsmen into smaller villages, where they
> are accommodated with neat dwelling-houses,
> each of them with an acre or two of land, to
> afford them the benefit of a milk cow.'

In other areas too, villages were being built for 'mechanicks' (tradesmen). One example of special interest today is the now-popular village of Grantown-on-Spey in Invernessshire. There, the minister records: (XVII, 556)

> 'Grantown is a village erected under the influence
> of the Grant family, it being little more than
> twenty years since the place where it stands was
> a poor rugged piece of heath. It now contains
> from 300 to 400 inhabitants, shoemakers, tailors,
> weavers of wool, linen and stockings,
> blacksmiths, wrights, masons and twelve
> merchants who keep regular shops in it.'

Another Highland village, Ullapool, also hugely popular today as a tourist resort, made its appearance around this time. We read that: (XVI, 41)

> 'The British (Fisheries) Society have fixed one of

their villages here. In this village there are now
about 72 houses, of which 35 are slated, the rest
are thatched with turf, fern roots and heather. The
principal inducement to settle in this village is its
advantageous situation for the herring fishing.'

Villages built specifically for tradesmen are perhaps to
be expected; altogether more surprising is the mention in
the account for Cargill in Perthshire of a special village
designed for ex-soldiers – surely a rare instance of
appreciation for military service: (XI, 60)

'It consists of about 80 dwelling-houses, with
necessary offices, built in a commodious manner
after a regular plan. To every house is annexed a
good garden, with about three acres of land
properly inclosed with hedge and ditch, and
sheltered with strips of planting.'

Providing poor people with gardens certainly represented
a real step forward. In contrast with the rich, their gardens
were scarcely worthy of the name. The general situation is
summed up by the writer of the Abernyte (Perthshire) report:
(XI,23)

'While the improvement of land in general has
been pretty well attended to, one branch of it, of
importance both to the pleasure and healthy
subsistence of the artisan, has been almost
entirely neglected, viz. gardening. In the gardens
even of the farmers, the only vegetables raised

are kail and potatoes, and sometimes a few
cabbages. In the cottager's yard, the last is
entirely omitted; though they are all fond of, and
consume great quantities of the onion tribe, they
never think of cultivating a single plant of them.'

Predictably, though, there are variations. Other accounts
mention leeks, carrots, 'collyflowers' and even artichokes. A
few tell of the beginnings of growing some soft fruits. The
report for Lamington in Lanarkshire for example has this:
(VII, 419)

'There is scarcely a garden which deserves the
name, as being almost without flowers, and
having little or no fruit except gooseberries,
currants and black berries.'

Interestingly, a very successful experiment in the growing
of rhubarb (highly regarded as an aperient) carried out by
the Duke of Atholl, heralded the production of this useful
root which would later be found in every cottage garden in
the land.

It cannot be stated too strongly that the liberality or
otherwise of the landed proprietors ('heritors') could and
did make a huge difference to the general wellbeing of the
poor. In a great many parishes, it seems only too clear that
the comfort of the people was the last thing on their minds;
in a few, however, there is heartening evidence of real care
and concern. One such shining example comes from the
parish of Urquhart in Inverness-shire. As this excerpt clearly

shows, the benign influence of Sir James Grant, the principal heritor, encompassed a great deal more than mere housing; what is noteworthy is that, while in many Highland parishes the number of listed poor could be as high as 100, in Glenurquhart none are recorded. There, agricultural improvements were proceeding apace: (XVII, 265)

> 'Sir James Grant gives rye-grass and clover seeds
> to the smaller tenants on his estate gratis. Most
> people have a small piece of land, which yields
> them the comforts of a milch cow.'

Not surprisingly, produce was plentiful:

> 'grain, potatoes, lint, hay, timber, black cattle,
> sheep, horses, goats, butter and cheese.'

Sufficient grain was actually produced to enable the people to export seed-oats and meal to surrounding districts. The lint production is explained by the fact that Sir James had built a lint-mill, so that:

> '. . . industry has been encouraged among the
> females, and both sexes exhibit on Sundays and
> holy-days, a much improved appearance, by now
> dressed in linen of their own manufacture.'

It is a truly cheering picture of the profound influence of a kindly landowner – one whose personal satisfaction and fulfilment must surely have been as great as that of his tenants. In this parish, then, there was obviously no shortage of food. In many others, though, there would be a dearth which could at times amount to famine. The years 1782-83 were a period of abject poverty. The minister of Tarbat in Easter Ross, for example, writes: (XVII,649)

> 'The spring of the year 1782 falls to be noticed
> for a scarcity of provender, and the ruin of many
> families both in the Highlands and the low
> country, by the loss of their cattle, as the
> consequence of that scarcity.'

He paints a sad picture of large numbers of poor being forced to beg for survival:

> 'Many came down to this and other parishes in
> search of provision for their families; and a pitiable
> case it was, to see persons young and otherwise
> vigorous in this condition, having hunger and
> distress of mind painted on their countenances.'

Some of the ministers write with gratitude of supplies of pease and oatmeal, sent by the government to relieve the poor. Others express their belief that the survival of the people has been providentially assured by immense numbers of shellfish and herring around the coasts, as well as unusually high milk yields in some areas. Thankfully, times as hard as this were rare.

When harvests were good, the outlook was of course altogether more favourable. Those Scots who had survived the hazards of childhood had indeed become renowned for their hardihood and health. Their working day could be anything up to 14 or 15 hours a day – no question in those days of low energy expenditure! As to the diet, while it was plain and simple and undoubtedly monotonous, its nutritional value was high, with the one outstanding failure lying in the scarcity of vegetables and virtual absence of fruit. The consequence was that scurvy, especially in winter and spring, was always a possibility. It is of interest to note that very few of the writers appear to have made any connection between the incidence of scurvy and paucity of vegetables, as a single example from Kinloss in Morayshire will show: (XVI, 620)

> 'The most prevalent distempers are cutaneous
> diseases, scurvy, and rheumatism, owing perhaps
> to hard labour, the sharpness of the air, a spare or
> fish diet, and want of cleanliness.'

Still, the people did have one bulwark against both hunger and the dreaded scurvy – the humble potato. In report after report, its praises are sung. All over Scotland, but especially in the Highlands and Islands, it becomes clear that dependence upon potatoes was growing all the time (to an extent, indeed, which would prove disastrous half a century later with the advent of the potato blight).

Possibly the most comprehensive account of the common people's food is that offered by the report from Speymouth in Morayshire, including not only a kind of menu but also a reference to the prime importance of potatoes: (XVI, 675)

> 'The diet of the labouring people here, and in
> general, is porridge, made of oatmeal, with milk

and beer, to breakfast; sowens (a kind of
flummery, made of oatmeal somewhat soured)
with milk and beer, to dinner: and kail, that is
greens or cabbage, boiled with oatmeal, to
supper. With all these, they use bread of oatmeal,
or what is called household meal, that is some
mixture of barley, rye and pease. On Sundays
they have generally barley broth, with some meat
in summer and butter in winter. In places near
the coast, they have sometimes fish. Turnips are
sometimes used in place of cabbage and greens;
and potatoes, dressed in various ways, with
butter, milk, onions etc., is commonly a third of
their food from the beginning of September to the
end of March.'

Potatoes, a third of their food? Not only so, but according
to some writers, much more! From Inishail in Argyll, as one
of many such comments, comes this: (VIII, 112)

'For nine months of the year, potatoes make a
great part of the food of the middling and lower
ranks of people.'

Similar claims are made from all over the country, along
with the highest possible praise for 'this most valuable root'.

In the reports from the Highlands and particularly the
Western Isles, a strong link is often made with another equally
valuable food – herrings. The only trouble was that
unfortunately herrings were capricious in their appearance,

but when huge shoals did come, their potential for sustenance was immense. Sadly, though, there was one great drawback – the lack of salt to preserve them. This scarcity, brought about through the hated Salt Tax, absolutely incensed the ministers (the word 'iniquitous' is often used) and many included a passionate appeal that it be repealed.

Just imagine people living on the edge of starvation being forced to throw back a huge catch of precious herrings! Yet this is exactly what happened in many places, as in the remote parish of Kintail: (XVII, 526)

> 'The take of herring from Lochduich was so immense, that a single boat killed six 'lasts' in a night; but when this source of wealth was at the door, the parishioners could find no supply (of salt), and some were necessitated to commit the herrings to their original bed.'

'If a barrel of salt might be distributed on oath,' suggests the Portree, Isle of Skye, minister (XX, 205),

> 'for the purpose of curing the relative quantity of herrings to be eaten with their potatoes, even one barrel would totally change the face of affairs, where subsistence is so scanty and population so overbearing. This trifling indulgence would contribute to the necessity of many thousands.'

The 'bread' used by the vast majority of Scots at the time was in the form of oatcakes, or bannocks, cooked on an iron girdle over the fire, since the ordinary folk had no ovens. In certain areas this was changing, and bakers were beginning to set up in business. Generally it is the accounts from more prosperous places which reflect a growing taste for wheaten bread. One such is that from Campsie in Stirlingshire: (IX, 274)

> 'The wheaten bread is now universally used by
> every description of people, there being no less
> than two bakers stationary within the parish,
> besides some hundred pounds of wheaten bread
> bought annually from Kirkintilloch and Glasgow.'

Much the same was true of meat, normally a luxury for ordinary folk and usually reserved for special domestic occasions such as baptisms, weddings and funerals. However, its use was increasing among the better-off tradesmen and in certain towns. In Kelso, for example, we read that: (V, 256)

> 'Although the mechanicks in town generally eat
> meat for dinner, the labourers in town and
> country seldom do so.'

But in Crieff and its surrounding villages, to which thousands of cattle converged in autumn for the great Trysts, not surprisingly we find that meat was enjoyed by all.

So much for the food. Clearly the twin dietary props were cereals and dairy products, along with potatoes, kail and turnips – augmented however by wild plants and fruits in season; fish for those within reach of the coasts, eggs, meat occasionally and a few pulses. It was a diet high in dairy fat when times were good, but almost entirely lacking in sugar – and thus altogether worthy of note today!

That food was often scarce cannot be denied, but in many areas another factor complicated the issue as well – the scarcity of fuel with which to cook it. From our own perspective of winter warmth and comfort, it requires an effort of imagination to picture something of the suffering endured by the poor through this single deficiency. In the whole of the Old Statistical Account, few subjects elicit stronger complaints on the part of the ministers.

'A human being pinched with cold,' says the recorder for Kirkinner in Galloway, 'when confined indoors, is always an inactive being. The daylight during the winter is spent by many of the women in gathering elding, as they call it, that is, sticks, furze and broom, for fuel; and the evening in warming their shivering limbs before the scanty fire which this produces.' (V, 424) What must it have been like, indeed, to possess the valuable staples, oatmeal and potatoes, and yet to be unable to cook them?

The grievances vary from area to area. In Perthshire, it is distance from coals; some parishes were 30-40 miles from coal, and one writer complains that 'half the summer is spent in bringing home as much coal as is necessary for the winter's supply.' All the same, whenever coal was to be had, the people wanted it.

In some coastal areas, notably Argyll, the principal grievance is the Coal Tax – hated just as much as the Salt Tax – levied on coal carried by sea.

'The heavy duty laid on coals carried coastwise, appears

to be as unreasonable as it is impolitic', maintains the Inveraray writer, 'and is universally complained of, and an intolerable burden.' (VIII, 139)

The writer from the Isle of Muck paints a miserable picture of occasions on which 'they were reduced to the necessity of burning different kinds of furniture, such as beds, dressers, stools, barrels, and also house timber, divots, tangles, straw etc., to dress their victuals'. Small wonder then that there was universal rejoicing when the iniquitous tax was finally repealed in 1793. None expresses this jubilation more vividly than the minister for Kilmuir Wester and Suddy: (XVII, 458)

> 'Every poor man's countenance here sparkled with
> joy, at being told of Mr Secretary Dundas's intention
> to bring a Bill this session into Parliament, to take
> the duty off coals coming to this country.'

When at last it happened, the minister for Borgue in the Borders had this to say: (V, 44)

> 'It is with no small pleasure, that the author of
> this account has just received intelligence, that
> the duty on coals is to be taken off. The
> advantages of this will be felt by all ranks; and it
> will scarcely admit of a doubt, that in a short time
> it will prove equally advantageous to the State.'

The allusion to the State refers to the belief expressed by some writers that the misery caused by lack of fuel has led many to emigrate.

'There is not one sensible man in Galloway', claims the

recorder from the parish of Urr, (V, 376) 'who will or can deny that if the tax on coals had been suppressed ten years ago, the king would have had 10,000 more subjects in the maritime part of the country.'

The difference made by ready access to fuel to the people's comfort and wellbeing is nowhere more apparent than in the Western Isles. There, virtually all the reports paint a distressing picture of cold, damp, cheerless houses. It therefore comes as a surprise to find in one account, that for Kilchoman in Islay, the comment that: (XX, 391)

> 'no country is better supplied with fire and water;
> almost every farm has peat moss within itself,
> affording charcoal for the smith, as we have no
> coals. These peats, and the fish oil we burn in
> lamps, make the habitation of the meanest
> cottages warm and cheery.'

The great difference which easy access to abundant supplies of peat made in this community is very clear; significantly, the writer goes on to tell of the people's love of dancing and playing the fiddle and bagpipes, as well as outdoor amusements such as shinty and putting the stone.

In other parishes, though, the winning of peats seems to have been much more difficult. A bleak comment comes from the account for Kilfinan in Argyll: (VIII, 230)

> 'The making, preparing and leading of peats
> consumes the greatest part of the people's time
> in summer; and too often, they lose the most of

them from the wetness of the climate, and the
softness of the roads.'

But in a caustic comment, the minister of Glenisla in
Angus prefers to blame the people: (XII, 283)

'They are not so industrious as could be wished.
The summer months are mostly spent in providing
fuel and tending the flocks; while the winter
months are mostly consumed in burning this fuel.'

However that may be, the picture of damp, dark, cold
houses is not an attractive one. Unsurprisingly, many of the
writers focus on the health hazards (and especially the great
prevalence of rheumatism) caused by these conditions.

Despite all the evidence of harsh living, it has to be said
that the picture from around Scotland presents much
diversity. Certainly in some of the more prosperous towns
there could be quite a considerable degree of comfort, and
even elegance and sophistication.

It is of interest, for example, to look closely at the lists of
local occupations which some of the writers offer; while in
the majority of rural parishes these comprise predominantly
agricultural labourers, weavers, blacksmiths, farmers, millers,
shoemakers and other tradesmen, in others (mainly near
the cities) a few very different ones can be found. Here is
the list from the parish of Inveresk near Edinburgh: (II, 301)

Bakers
Carters
Fishermen

Fishwives
Fleshers
Gardeners
Grocers
Hairdressers
Mantua Makers
Masons
Milliners
Perfumers
Salt Wives
Shoemakers
Tailors
Weavers
Winemakers

Arguably the most genteel picture comes from Montrose, where we read of: (XIII, 560)

'social visits at all seasons, a monthly club for gentlemen, exhibitions to gratify curiosity and increase knowledge, golf, bowls, billiards, cards, shooting, and winter assemblies conducted with the utmost decorum.'

And the country town of Banff boasts a town house which has two drawing rooms, where 'during the winter season, there are dancing assemblies once a fortnight'.

One extract to illustrate an altogether more elegant aspect

of Scottish lifestyle in a more favoured area is from the
account for Kirkmichael (Banff): (XVI, 307)

> 'Formerly the hair flowed in easy ringlets over the
> shoulders; not many years ago, it was bound
> behind with a cue; now it spreads into a
> protuberance on the forehead, supported by
> cushions; sometimes it is plain, and split in the
> middle. But who can describe the caprice of
> female ornament, more various than the changes
> of the moon?'

'For weddings, a fiddler or two, and perhaps a boy
to scrape on an old violoncello, are engaged'

CHAPTER 4

Customs

TO THOSE blessed with a keen sense of history there can be few things more satisfying than ferreting out details of how our ancestors lived, what were their commonly-held beliefs, and perhaps especially, how they celebrated the important events of domestic and social life such as births, marriages and deaths. Trawling through the old parish accounts can thus be a fascinating exercise.

The comments of some writers on funeral customs, for example, highlight the tragically high death rate among infants and children at the time. 'Of all children born', says the minister of Aberfoyle, 'more than one half die before the age of ten years' (XII, 9); while the report for Collington, Edinburgh offers actual figures: 'Of the 944 persons buried, 452, or nearly one half, were children under 14 years of age.' (II, 139)

The difficulty of arriving at accurate mortality figures is emphasised by some. For a start, many children were not registered because of the expense involved, as the report for Eccles makes clear: (III, 156)

> 'There are more baptisms than those which are
> registered,; but of late years, since the tax of
> threepence was paid to the king, over and above

the usual fees of registration, many cannot be
prevailed upon to register their children's names.'

Another difficulty was that records were based mainly
on use of the 'mort-cloth' (funeral pall), the rental of which
provided one of the main sources of poor relief; but as its
use was generally reserved for those over ten years old, and
denied to paupers, true figures were understandably hard to
ascertain.

Those eligible to use the mort-cloth, however, were
expected to do so; thus the consternation caused in the
following instance from the minister of Newton in the
Lothians may well be imagined: (II, 365)

'The colliers purchased a set of mort-cloths, the
use of which was given, gratis, to the contributors.
The body of carters, who have a great fund of the
same kind, followed their example. As the great
body of the parish consists of these two
descriptions of people, the kirk-session foresaw
that this practice, if allowed to continue, would
soon go nearly to extinguish altogether the funds
arising from the use of the mort-cloths.'

The matter was indeed serious, for there were many on
the poor's list, the only other resource coming from the (often
meagre) collections at the church door, or sometimes interest
on charitable bequests. (A heritors' tax based on land owner-
ship did exist in a few places). In Newton the mort-cloth
affair went eventually to law, and the Court of Session ruled

that the use of any except parish mort-cloths should be forbidden.

Customs connected with funerals receive considerable attention in the parish reports. An unusual one comes from Borrowstownness (Bo'ness); it is clearly a survival from medieval times, the beadle taking the place of the old town-crier: (II, 712)

> 'At the burials of the poor people, a custom, almost obsolete in other parts of Scotland, is continued here. The beadle perambulates the streets with a bell, and intimates the death of the individual in the following language: 'All brethren and sisters, I let ye to wit, there is a brother (or sister) departed at the pleasure of the Almighty (here he lifts his hat) called _____. All those that come to the burial come at __ o'clock. The corpse is at _____. He also walks before the corpse to the churchyard, ringing his bell.'

In the far north, Tongue in Sutherland has its own distinctive and respectful way of conducting funerals. 'Burials are conducted in this parish with great decorum', claims the minister: (XVIII, 481)

> 'None, even of the common people, attend without a particular invitation. After some entertainment [hospitality] (for at the burial of the poorest here, there is refreshment given, consisting generally of whisquybeath, or some foreign liquor, butter and

cheese and oat bread), the friends of the deceased, and neighbours of the village, who come to witness the interment, are drawn up in rank and file by an old serjeant, or some veteran who has been in the army and who attends to maintain order, and give, as they term it here, the word of relief. Upon his crying Relief!, the four under the bier prepare to leave their stations and make room for another four, that instantly succeed. This progression is observed, at the interval of every five minutes, till the whole attendants come in regularly; and if the distance requires it, there is a second, a third, or a fourth round of such evolutions gone through. When the persons present are not inflamed with liquor (which is now seldom the case) there is a profound silence generally observed from the time the corpse has been taken up, till the interment is over.'

The hospitality offered in the parish of Dundonald in Ayrshire is rather different. 'Country burials are not well regulated', claims the writer: (VI, 178)

'The company are invited at 11 o'clock forenoon, but they are, probably, not all arrived at two. Till of late a pipe and tobacco were provided for everyone of the company, but this custom is laid aside.'

Interestingly, it seems that the Joneses were around even in the eighteenth century! Many of the ministers are clearly concerned that the excessive expense incurred by bereaved families will lead to very negative consequences. Inordinate expense is the main concern of the minister of Carmunnock when he writes: (VII, 173)

'It is usual in this parish, as in many other parts of Scotland, when a death has taken place, to invite on such occasions the greater part of the country around; and though called to attend at an early hour in the forenoon, yet it is generally towards evening, before they think of carrying forth the corpse to the churchyard for interment. While, on these occasions, the good folk are assembled, though they never run into excess, yet no small expense is incurred by the family; who often vie with those around them in giving, as they call it, an honourable burial to their deceased friend. Such a custom is attended with many evils and frequently involves debt, or reduces to poverty, many families otherwise frugal and industrious, by this piece of useless parade and ill-judged expense.'

Another minister who writes critically of excessive funeral expenses is from the parish of Dunlop in Ayrshire: (VI, 192)

'The only custom which the people may be said to retain is that of having great and expensive burials. It is no unusual thing when a wealthy person dies, to invite two or three parishes to

attend his funeral; and as they are limited to no
particular hour, a great part of the day is taken up
in coming to it, and waiting on it. But the loss of
labour, and the loss of time, are not the only evils
that follow it; it becomes oppressive to those
who cannot afford the expense, but who, from
vanity or pride, must continue the custom.'

The accent on the loss of labour is unusual; yet indeed
with mourners coming from a wide area and mainly on foot,
this must certainly have caused considerable disruption in a
farming community. All the same, in the majority of reports
it is the potential consequence of family debt which seems
to cause the most concern.

While most ministers write with fairly mild censure, the
one penning the report for the parish of Kilmaurs, again in
Ayrshire, has a more acid tone; his concern, also, is more
for the living than the dead: (VI, 334)

'No unusual customs prevail among the
inhabitants of the parish. There is one indeed
common to the whole country, that of gathering
many people together, and entertaining them at
considerable expense when they bury their dead.
However ill it can be afforded, nothing must be
spared that custom has sanctioned. By exploding
this in a great measure, many would have it in
their power to do more essential acts of kindness
to their friends and relations while living. There is
little merit in helping to bury those whom we

help to starve. Nor do the deceased feel or enjoy any of the gratifications of vanity or misplaced veneration, which prompt to this custom.'

In a note on funeral customs, an excerpt from the report from Borthwick, Lothians is of interest, especially since it could be said to have, at least to some extent, survived to this day: (II, 78)

'According to a prejudice of very ancient date, the common wish is to be buried with our fathers; and from the change of residence, which ever must take place among the great body of the people, and the fluctuating state of all human affairs, there are not above two farmers in these bounds who bury in this place. They carry their deceased friends elsewhere: and, in return, the dead are bought here from neighbouring parishes, and sometimes from a very considerable distance.'

When it comes to looking at marriage customs, one thing is immediately apparent – while almost everything in relation to lifestyle has changed almost beyond recognition between the late eighteenth century and today, one thing most certainly has not; every bride now as then wants to wear her best on this special day. The fact that young women scrimped and saved to buy a wedding gown, however, displeased the ministers. True, they probably had good reasons – poverty-stricken folk would undoubtedly have had more pressing

necessities on which to spend their money – but it is the
snobbish attitude of the writers which often comes across,
as in this example from the Dunoon account: (VIII, 93)

> 'The scarlet cloak, that only covered the
> shoulders of our ladies fifty years ago, now falls
> to the heels of our servant maids, and many of
> them purchase a silk gown to be married in.'

Let no maidservant dare to aspire to a silk gown!

One of the most noteworthy customs was of course the
irregular 'trade' carried on at Gretna, referred to by the local
minister as 'a disgrace to the police of a civilised country'.

At least as much ministerial ire is called forth on the
subject of what was known as the Penny Bridal. It has to be
said, all the same, that these very common weddings seem
to have had two sides. On one hand it is apparent that they
could present, as some accounts suggest, 'scenes of
excessive revelry and drunkenness'; on the other, they must
have represented a great deal of communal goodwill and
even sacrificial giving, since whatever hospitality was
dispensed usually came from neighbours and friends. They
must also have been a kind of oasis in a life too often
characterised by grinding poverty and unremitting toil.

One example comes from Ross-shire: (Avoch, XVII, 324)

> 'Marriages, in this place, are generally conducted in
> the style of Penny Bridals. Little other fare is
> provided except bread, ale or whisky. The relatives,
> who assemble in the morning, are entertained with

a dram and drink gratis. But, after the ceremony is performed, every man pays for his drink. The neighbours then convene in great numbers. A fiddler or two, and perhaps a boy to scrape on an old violoncello, are engaged. A barn is allotted for the dancing and a house for the drinking. And thus they make merry for two or three days.'

A variation on the theme comes from Methlick in Aberdeenshire: (XV, 318)

'They are a social people; as one evidence of their being so, there may be sometimes 60, 70, and sometimes 100 at a wedding, to the expense of which the guests contribute, by sending some milk, butter, cheese, poultry, etc.'

One cannot help wondering whether it may have been in anticipation of 'excessive revelry' that this writer adds that the guests also 'send stone plates and jugs'!

It is with some surprise that one finds reference to young men marrying for money, but this seems indeed to have happened in the parish of Liff and Bervie in Angus: (XIII, 395)

'In cases of marriage here, it often happens that the man is far less advanced in life than the woman he marries. The former depends very much on the experience of the latter, and generally too on the savings of her industry, to enable him to begin with some comfort a married life.'

The writer passes no judgement on this somewhat cynical practice, merely adding that 'the disparity of years happening on the side of the woman, must needs be a hindrance to population'.

Another surprising comment regarding marriage customs comes from the Western Isles. In the report for Stornoway we read: (XX, 38)

> 'The common people of this island marry very early; and when death separates them, if the surviving party, whether male or female, finds it convenient to engage a second or third time in that state, some of them remain only a few weeks, and some only a few days, in widowhood; so that grief for the loss of husband or wife is an affliction little known among the lower class of people here. A woman in this country, whose husband shot himself accidentally by an unguarded management of a firelock, settled her contract of marriage, in the way she saw fit, before the body of her late husband was interred, and was married the next day after she performed the last duty to the deceased.'

Frequently in reading these old parish accounts one is left wondering whether the ministers' remarks are intended to be humorous, and this is one such from the account for Walls & Sandness in Shetland:

> 'One reason why few men remain unmarried is

because, if not married, they are sure to be fixed
upon by the landmasters, for the service of the
navy, when a draft for that service is required
from the country; and rather than be forced from
their native soil, and the society of their friends,
they will submit to many inconveniences.'

Baptisms might have been expected to have been occasions for celebrations in a similar manner to marriages and funerals; instead, the few comments made are centred on superstitious practices, as in this extract from the Logierait, Perthshire, account: (XII, 712)

'When a child was baptised privately, it was long
since customary, to put the child upon a clean
basket, having a cloth previously spread over it,
with bread and cheese put into the cloth; and
thus to move the basket three times successively
round the iron crook which hangs over the fire.'

'Those who complain of rheumatism in the back, must ascend the hill,
then lie down on their back, and be pulled by the legs to the bottom.
This operation is still performed, and reckoned very efficacious.'

CHAPTER 5

Superstitions

THOSE ALREADY familiar with the Old Statistical Account must surely have noticed a wide diversity of views on almost every subject – from the big issues like agricultural improvements and the desirability of industrial development to domestic matters like suitable dress for maidservants.

This is not to say that the Old Statistical Account does not present a true picture of Scottish life in the late eighteenth century; of course it does, for it comes, as it were, straight from the horse's mouth. It's just that there were 938 horses!

It is not surprising to find distinct differences in perception among the writers when it comes to a subject as sensitive as superstitious practices. In fact the accounts seem to fall naturally into three distinct groups – those who deny the existence of all paranormal experience; those who allow that superstition exists, but is on its way out; and those who write frankly about what are clearly-held beliefs in their parishes. And there are a large number of accounts in which the subject is not mentioned at all. It might well have been that each writer reflected exactly what was prevalent in his own area. On the other hand some ministers may have been more aware than others of the superstitious beliefs of their flocks.

Perhaps strongest of all in his denial of the paranormal (and most determined to relegate all such folly to a past, less enlightened age) is the minister of Montquhitter in Aberdeenshire, who produced an outstanding report. (XV, 346)

> 'An amazing alteration has been brought about by education and social intercourse. Few of the old being able to read, and fewer still to write, their minds were clouded by ignorance. The mind being now cultivated, the imagination readily admitted the terrors of superstition. The appearance of ghosts and demons too frequently engrossed the conversation of the young and the old.'

But now all this foolishness is apparently a thing of the past.

> 'In the minds of the young, cultivated by education, a steady pursuit of the arts of life has banished the chimeras of fancy.'

The writer from the parish of Clunie in Perthshire takes a similar view: (XII, 244)

> 'They are not, as formerly, the dupes of superstitious credulity. Many old useless rites and ceremonies are laid aside. Little attention is paid to bug-bear tales; superstitions, charms, incantations, have lost their power. Cats, hares, magpies, and old women, cease to assume any other appearance than what nature has given them; and ghosts, goblins, witches, and fairies have relinquished the land.'

The same seems to hold true for the parish of Kilfinan in

Argyll: 'Superstition is losing ground here pretty fast'. But here the minister is prepared to cite one exception: (VIII, 235)

> 'There is one practice that prevails much in this parish, which took its rise from this source; which is, the carrying out to baptism the first or second day after birth. Many of them, although they had it in their option to have their children baptised in their own houses, by waiting a day, prefer carrying them seven or eight miles to church, in the worst weather of December or January, by which folly they too often sacrifice their children to the phantom of superstition.'

In the account for Mid-Calder in the Lothians, there is a similar belief that 'the darkness of error' is passing, but with one important exception: (II, 106)

> 'It behoves us to rejoice that we live in happier times, when the darkness of error is giving way to the light of reason, truth and science. As this darkness is removed, so will those opinions, prejudices, and spectres die, to which ignorance and folly gave birth. I cannot say that the belief in witchcraft has entirely left the people in this parish; but it appears to have little influence in their lives or their conduct. May the human mind daily increase in wisdom, and assert more and more its native dignity, till it rise superior to folly, superstition and vice.'

In a few cases we find interesting relics of superstition which have a unique origin, as in this report from Canisbay in Caithness: (XVIII, 23)

> 'No gentleman of the name Sinclair, either in Canisbay or throughout Caithness, will put on green apparel, or think of crossing the Ord upon a Monday. They were dressed in green, and they crossed the Ord upon a Monday on their way to the battles of Flowden [Flodden], where they fought and fell in the service of their country, almost without leaving a representative of the name behind them. The day and the dress are accordingly regarded as inauspicious.'

The minister of Foxglen in Angus is aware of many superstitious beliefs, even though he believes they are passing. 'The superstition of former times is now much worn out,' he writes: (XVI, 179)

> 'There remains, however, still a little. Some charms are secretly used to prevent evil; and some omens looked to by the older people. There are happy and unhappy days for beginning any undertaking. Thus, few would choose to be married here on a Friday, though it is the ordinary day in other quarters of the church. There are also happy and unhappy feet. Thus, they wish bridegrooms and brides a happy foot; and to prevent any bad effect, they salute those whom they meet on the road with a kiss.'

The writer finishes his piece with a touch of humour:

> 'It is hard, however, if any misfortune happens
> when you are passing, that you should be
> blamed, when neither you nor your feet ever
> thought of the matter.'

Another report which recounts a rather strange super-stitious belief comes from Kilfinichen and Kilviceuen in Mull: (XX, 321)

> 'They are by no means superstitious, yet they still
> retain some opinions handed down by their
> ancestors, perhaps from the time of the druids. It
> is believed by them, that the spirit of the last
> person that was buried watches round the
> churchyard till another is buried, to whom he
> declines his charge.'

It seems surprising that little is written about the treatment of disease by herbal means, although in fact the following excerpt from the Perthshire parish of Abernyte makes one wonder whether, alongside (or possibly instead of) what the minister describes as 'spells and charms', herbs may have been in use. 'Belief in the power of spells and charms still prevails here in a great degree,' he writes: (XI, 30)

> 'They attribute power to them only in internal
> disorders and some chronical diseases. A
> knowledge of them is confined to a few families.
> The recourse of the people to remedies of this
> kind is less to be wondered at, as they are at a

distance from a regular practitioner in physic.'

This writer is doubtful as to the rapid passing of superstitious practice and belief. 'It must be a considerable amount
of time', he affirms, 'before every species of superstition be
eradicated from the minds of people who consider everything
as sacred that has been sanctioned by the belief of their
fathers.'

One who would certainly have agreed is the writer from
Applecross in Ross-shire: (XVII, 294)

> 'There are none of the common calamities, or
> distressful accidents incident to man or beast, but
> hath its particular charm or incantation; these are
> generally made up of a group of unconnected
> words, and an irregular address to the Deity, or to
> some one of the saints. The desire for health, and
> the power of superstition, reconciled many to the
> use of them; nor are they as yet, among the
> lower class, wholly fallen into disuse. With them
> the belief of the second sight is general, and the
> power of the evil eye is fully credited; and though
> the faith in witchcraft be much enfeebled, the
> virtue of abstracting the substance from one milk,
> and adding it to another is rarely questioned.'

Another who attributes superstition principally to 'the
lower class' is the writer from Kirkwall and St Ola in Orkney:
(XIX, 144)

> 'Many of the lower class are still so ignorant as to
> be under the baneful influence of superstition. In

many days of the year they will neither go to the
sea in search of fish, nor to perform any sort of
work at home. . . On going to sea, they would
reckon themselves in the most imminent danger,
were they by accident to turn their boat in
opposition to the sun's course.'

A few of the common beliefs are nothing if not bizarre;
this one from South Ronaldsay also displays a touch of male
chauvinism: (XIX, 194)

'Within these last seven years, the minister has
been twice interrupted in administering baptism
to a female child before the male child, who was
baptised immediately after. When the service was
over he was gravely told that he had done very
wrong, for as the female child was first baptised
she would, on coming to the years of discretion,
most certainly have a strong beard, and the boy
would have none.'

The minister then goes on to describe other, more sinister
practices:

'The existence of faeries and witches is seriously
believed by some, who, in order to protect
themselves, draw imaginary circles and place
knives in the walls of houses. The worst
consequence of this superstition is that, when a
person loses a horse or cow, it sometimes
happens that a poor woman in the
neighbourhood is blamed, and knocked in some

part of the head, above the breath, until blood
appears. But there are many decent, honest, and
sensible people, who laugh at such absurdities.'

Laughing at such things was all very well, but from several accounts it is clear that this touches on what was undoubtedly the most worrying aspect – the dangers to which certain old women were exposed, especially if they had the misfortune to have a certain cast of features, or even keep a cat. Doubtless there were some who did dabble in occult practices; for the many who were innocent though, this must have caused considerable fear and distress.

The minister of Kirkmichael (Angus) has plenty to say about superstition, and writes in a spirit of irony or downright contempt: (XVI, 296)

'It may easily be imagined that this country has its
due proportion of that superstition which generally
prevails over the Highlands. Poor Martin Scriblerus
never more anxiously watched the blowing of the
wind to secure an heir to his genius, than the love-
sick swain and his nymph for the coming of the
new moon to be noosed together in matrimony.
Should the planet happen to be at the height of her
splendour when the ceremony is performed, their
life together will be a scene of festivity, and all its
paths strewed over with rose-buds of delight. But
when her tapering horns are turned towards the
North, passion becomes frost-bound, and seldom
thaws until the genial season again approaches.'

Next he turns to belief in ghosts:

> 'On the sequestered hill, and in the darksome
> valley, frequently does the benighted traveller
> behold the visionary semblance of his departed
> friend, perhaps of his enemy. Not more firmly
> established in this country is the belief in ghosts,
> than that in faeries.'

Finally he turns his attention to witches:

> 'Even at present, witches are supposed as of old
> to ride on broomsticks through the air. They
> make fields barren or fertile, raise or still
> whirlwinds, give or take away milk at pleasure.
> The force of their incantations is not to be
> resisted, and extends even to the moon in her
> aerial career.'

It is difficult to deny the conclusion that, taken as a whole, there was still a great deal of occult belief and practice in Scotland at the end of the eighteenth century. The minister from Montquhitter in Aberdeenshire (with whose report we began this section) is having none of it. To him, all such nonsense belongs to a past age:

> 'But now, ghosts and demons are no longer
> visible. Faeries, without requiring compensation,
> have renounced their possessions. The sagacious
> old woman, who has survived her friends and
> means, is treated with humanity, in spite of the
> grisly bristles which adorn her mouth.'

His parting shot is against those – mainly the upper classes – who have turned to scepticism and unbelief:

> 'From believing too much many, particularly in
> the higher walks of life, have rushed to the
> opposite extreme of believing too little; so that,
> even in this remote corner, scepticism may justly
> boast of her votaries.'

In pre-Reformation times there had been widespread veneration of certain wells in Scotland; later this was frowned upon and actively discouraged. In the Old Statistical Account, three distinct kinds of wells receive mention. Some clearly go back to pagan times; some are associated with the name of a saint; some, generally 'chalybeate' springs (i.e. containing iron) were believed to have therapeutic properties – forerunners no doubt to the popular spas of the nineteenth century.

The 'clootie well' in Avoch on the Black Isle, of pagan origin and festooned with pieces of cloth ('cloots') is still to be seen there. The writer for Avoch describes it thus: (XVII, 301)

> 'A well called Craiguck, issuing from a rock near the
> shore of Bennetsfield, is resorted to in the month of
> May, by whimsical or superstitious people, who,
> after drinking, commonly leave some threads or
> rags tied to a bush in the neighbourhood. But if they
> derive benefit from this, it would seem to be more
> owing to their own credulity, than to any effect of
> the water, which differs nothing in taste or
> appearance from common.'

Another well with a history reaching back to pagan times is mentioned at some length in the account for the Island of Gigha: (XX, 28)

> 'It would be unpardonable not to mention the well of Tarbat, a well famous for having command of the wind. Six feet above where the water gushes out there is a heap of stones, which forms a cover to the sacred fount. When a person wished for a fair wind, this part was opened with great solemnity, the stones carefully removed, and the well cleaned with a wooden dish or clam shell. This being done, the water was several times thrown in the direction from which the wished-for wind was to blow, and this action accompanied with a certain form of words, which the person repeated every time he threw the water. This ceremony of 'cleaning the well', as it is called, is now seldom or never performed; though still there are two old women, who are said to have the secret, but who have cause to lament the infidelity of the age, as they derive little emolument from their profession.'

Legends concerning St Fillan abound in a certain area of Perthshire. One description of a well connected with the saint is recorded in the Comrie account: (XII, 271)

> 'The only remarkable spring here is that of St Fillan, the popish saint of Breadalbane and Stratherne. The invalids, whether men, women,

> or children, walk or are carried round the well in
> a direction of DEISHAL, i.e. from east to west
> according to the course of the sun. They also
> drink of the water, and bathe in it.'

Here too the 'clootie' tradition held sway; the invalids threw a white stone on to the cairn of the saint, as well as leaving behind as tokens of gratitude rags of linen or woollen cloth. The writer describes another fearsome-sounding kind of 'therapy' – a rough attempt at traction, perhaps, but surely more painful than the disease:

> 'The rock on the summit of the hill formed of
> itself a chair for the saint, which still remains.
> Those who complain of rheumatism in the back,
> must ascend this hill, then lie down on their
> back, and be pulled by the legs to the bottom of
> the hill. This operation is still performed, and
> reckoned very efficacious.'

It seems clear that in the more prosperous towns, e.g. Montrose and Banff on the east coast, 'taking the waters' had already become fairly common. The writer of the Banff account has this to say: (XVI, 45)

> 'They sometimes place as much dependence on
> the quantity, as on the quality, of the water. Having
> but little time to spare for the fashionable
> avocations of a watering-place, they are very
> diligent during their stay, and are often known to
> swallow three gallons a day of the salutiferous
> stream, besides a reasonable portion of sea-water.'

(It is hard to avoid the thought that these patients must have been at least as robust in their desire to get well as those who allowed themselves to be dragged down the hill at Comrie.)

Another famous well – this time from a chalybeate spring – is described at some length by the Peterhead writer. Many people came in summer, not only for sea-bathing but also to chew certain seaweeds; so popular was the well that 'by six or seven in the morning, the spring is often literally dry'. Small wonder, perhaps, that it appears to have been a real panacea: (XV, 425)

> 'long deservedly in repute for the general debility, disorders of the stomach and bowels, flatulences and indigestion, nervous complaints which flow from these causes, and diseases peculiar to the fair sex.'

The writer has grave doubts, however, about its efficacy in the case of 'gravel' (or kidney/bladder stones), citing the case of a 42 year old sedentary man, whose grandfather and great-grandfather died of this complaint:

> 'He is thinking of trying the Peterhead water, because his father thought he derived benefit from it, who, after having tried it for nearly 30 years, was cut for the stone.'

Finally, there is the enigmatic story of the ailing Englishman who arrived at the famous well near Kirkconnell suffering from scurvy and 'emaciated, bowed down, feeble and dispirited' and went away 'stout and lively and joyous' after drinking the waters of the well.

'The state of the roads in this parish may be considered as a
disadvantage, being almost in a state of nature. . .'

CHAPTER 6

Grievances

WHEN Sir John Sinclair conceived his ambitious plan to produce this remarkable collection of facts, figures and commentary, his purpose was to a large extent altruistic. His expressed wish was that demonstration of both strengths and weaknesses around the entire country should 'add to the quantum of happiness' of the ordinary people.

Was this aim accomplished? Historians differ in their views; many are likely to say that it failed. It can at least be claimed, however, that a real opportunity was offered to the ministers – who knew their parishioners and local conditions better than anybody – to air their grievances. And of these there was certainly no lack!

Many of the commonest ones are raised time and again – as for example scarcity of fuel, forced labour, short leases, crumbling churches and manses, exploitation of the school-masters, oppression by the press-gangs. But now and again one comes across totally individual complaints, of which arguably none is more justifiable than this one from the minister of Barra in the Western Isles: (XX, 135)

> 'The compilers of the Encyclopaedia Britannica
> will do well to correct their error in calling Barra a

> rock half a mile in circumference, inhabited by
> solan geese [gannets] and other wild fowls.'

Certainly finding oneself wiped off the map must have been more than a little disconcerting! One cannot help wondering whether an apology was forthcoming.

It is of course well known that emigration had been taking place long before this time. It is still of much interest to look for evidence of such, especially of forced emigration, in this final decade of the eighteenth century, some forty or fifty years before the more notorious clearances took place in the Highlands.

From the Highland parish of Creich comes this comment, typical of many: (XVIII, 337)

> 'In the year 1772-73, several emigrated to
> America. Some farms have been conjoined, and
> a considerable number of tenants have been
> removed, out of grounds turned into sheep-
> walks. By all these means, the people have been
> considerably diminished.'

It is the familiar story of sheep being preferred to people, although admittedly without the barbarity of some of the evictions of the nineteenth century.

A fuller and more revealing description by the minister from South Uist offers an explanation for the mass emigration from that island: (XX, 117)

> 'From 1772-73, several thousands emigrated
> from the Western Islands to America, among

whom were more than 200 from here. . . The sense of grievance, whether real or imaginary; the fear of having the fruits of their industry called for by the landlords, many of whom think they have a right to the tenants' earnings except what barely supports life; want of employment for such as have no land to cultivate, and the facility of procuring a property for a small sum of money, the produce of which they can call their own, and from which their removal does not depend on the will of capricious masters. These are the principal motives that determine people now to emigrate to America, without at all attending to the difficulties and discouragements in their way, arising from the danger they must encounter in crossing the seas.'

In addition to outlining these factors leading to emigration, this minister offers his own recommendations for stopping this drift overseas. 'To put a stop to the present rage for emigration', he writes, 'requires very nice management in the proprietors.' They should therefore:

1. Renew the old attachment between them and the people.
2. Grant long leases.
3. Help with improvements, giving 'premiums' to the most deserving.
4. Establish 'manufactures'.
5. Erect villages.

All undoubtedly excellent ideas, but with a slim chance of being carried out! Some of the worst accounts of oppression by landlords come from the Western Isles.

In the Northern Isles, reports such as this one asserted by the minister of Firth and Stenness tend to concentrate rather on an altogether different kind of migration: (XIX, 93)

> 'Nothing contributes so much to the hurt of this place as the resort of the Hudson's Bay Company's ships to Stromness, and their engaging lads from this country. A few lads returning with some money make excellent recruits for the Company's service; and the report of a war makes great numbers solicit to go out to their settlements. The farmers' sons and servants leave them, to spend the prime of life in cold and drudgery in the North-West; and whence such of them as are not incapacitated by diseases contracted there, return to be farmers, their skill in that line not improved by their absence. . . Young lads, however, who have married before they have any stock, are able to remit a trifle to their families.'

The minister ends his comments by recording an unexpected benefit arising from the situation:

> 'When a man and his wife cannot live in peace together, the parties and the parish are relieved from such disquiets, by the husband's retreat to

the Hudson Bay's settlements.'

While some of the writers seem to accept emigration without expressing regret, others write emotionally about the loss of the people from their parishes. One such is the minister from Strachur and Strathlachlan in Argyll: (VIII, 417)

> 'The district is now thinned of its inhabitants. The people have been forced to leave their native hills. The sheep have banished the men. Where, in 12 or 16 families, a hardy race was reared, an opulent tacksman, with a shepherd or two, occupy the lands. The Highlanders of old did not live either in plenty or in elegance, yet they were happy. They were passionately fond of music and poetry. The song and the dance soon made them forget their toils. The sound of bagpipes is now seldom heard. With the modes of life that nourished it, the vein for poetry has now disappeared. The deer have fled from the mountains. A forest, in the close neighbourhood of this parish, where several hundreds of them roamed at pleasure, is now converted into sheep-walk.'

One particularly interesting comment comes from the report for Walls and Flota in Orkney: (XIX, 344)

> 'What accounts for an increase in population here is the settlement of a colony of Highlanders, who had been forced to emigrate from Strathnaver, where their farms were converted into sheep

pastures. These people, it would appear, had
been comfortably situated in their former
residence, as they all brought with them to this
place, a very considerable stock in horses, cows,
sheep, and goats, and also in grain.'

No doubt those displaced felt aggrieved by the loss of
their homes in Sutherland; in view of the brutal clearances
of the following century, though, we now know them to have
been the fortunate ones.

Moving on to look at other common grievances, we find a
great many references to the condition of the roads –
described as anything from poor to appalling. A useful
description comes from the pen of the Humbie minister,
showing that at last the situation is beginning to improve:
(II, 508)

'Before the year 1770, the roads were so bad,
that in many places they were impassable in
winter, and at no season of the year could more
than five bolls of grain be sent to market upon a
two-horse cart. But in consequence of an Act of
Parliament for the country, levying 20s. for every
ploughgate of land, they are now in so good
repair that 10 bolls are the common load.'

In many (indeed probably most) other places, the scene
was very different – for example as described in this report
from Errol in Perthshire: (XI, 177)

'The parish has always had a bad name for roads.
In a wet country, and deep soil, the track either of
man or beast, when much used and never
repaired, soon becomes unpleasant, if not
impassable.'

And from Ettrick in the Borders comes this complaint:
(III, 678)

'This parish possesses no advantage. The nearest
market town is 15 miles distant. The only road
that looks like a turnpike is to Selkirk; but even it
in many places is so deep, as greatly to obstruct
travelling. The distance is about 16 miles, and it
requires four hours to ride it.'

It is not surprising that most of the roads in the Western
Isles receive gloomy reports, the chief complaint often being
the woeful lack of bridges. The account for the Small Isles is
typical: (XX, 250)

'The state of the roads in this parish may be
considered as a disadvantage, being almost in a
state of nature. . . There is not a bridge in the
whole parish, yet it is obvious, that small ones
are absolutely necessary in Eigg and Rum, as
several of our waters become often dangerous,
by heavy falls of rain, and melting of snow.'

In Mull, the minister speaks from personal experience:
(XX, 284)

'It is dangerous for travellers to attempt to cross
them either a-foot or on horseback, and often they
cannot be crossed either way. The incumbent has
crossed them both a-foot and on horseback, often
at great risk, and has been stopped by them for 2
hours more than once, though within a few miles
of his own house. There have been a few persons
lost in these rivers.'

It would appear from most accounts that generally
speaking the military roads are the only ones worthy of
praise, although occasionally a fairly new turnpike road is
an exception. The account of Sorbie is of interest here: (V,
511)

'Good roads are of high importance in improving
a country. Wherever they are made, all obstacles
are surmounted, and the improvement of every
field capable of it, follows as a certain
consequence. The military road from Dumfries
and Portpatrick has produced many good effects
in this respect. By means of it, mountains
formerly appearing impervious are now no longer
formidable. The stranger passes with ease, to
give and receive information; and articles of trade
are transported with facility. The road making
from this country to Edinburgh, by a nearer way
than Dumfries, and that into Airshire through the
mountains, must be followed by the best
consequences.'

If bad roads were a cause for complaint, so indeed were poor harbours. In a full account setting out the main reasons for the decline of the fishing industry, the writer from Benholme, Kincardineshire cites the lack of good harbours, along with the oppression of the press-gangs, as responsible for the vessel owners having transferred to Montrose. On the activities of the press gangs he has this to say: (XIV, 41)

> 'As the boats were returning from the sea in 1756, a tender intercepted three of them, and impressed the stoutest of their men. A demand from government of every fifth man to serve on board the fleet followed. The fishers were obliged to comply with the necessity of the times, by either going themselves or bribing others in their stead; and thus purchased protections for those who remained, at great expense. Reduced in men and money, they were unable, by the end of the war in 1763, to fit out more than eight large boats, and as many small. In 1768, they were oppressed by press gangs, and forced to raise a new levy, at the rate of £10 or £12 a man. Distressed by so many demands, and deprived of the means of supplying them, many stout young men abandoned the fishing, and bound themselves apprentices to colliers, in order to avoid serving in the navy.'

This is altogether a sad story. Judging by the description of the conditions endured by the miners as told in the account for Alloa, they were escaping from one set of horrors to another. There, it was estimated: (IX, 680)

> 'a diligent bearer often brings in, from the bottom
> of the pit, six chalders, or nine tons of coal in the
> week.'

And many of those bearers were women and children!

In reports from fishing areas, the Salt Tax is frequently mentioned as a source of hardship, leading in some cases to catches having to go to waste through scarcity of salt.

Not surprisingly, many of the ministers complain of the poor state of their churches and manses. Some of them resort to sarcasm in their reports, as in this one from Glasford in Lanarkshire: (VII, 278)

> 'The church was built in 1663. It never was
> elegant or convenient. Its present uncouth
> appearance fixes the attention of every beholder,
> and scarce a stranger passes by without making it
> a compliment. It is not in good repair. The
> heritors, unlike the ancient Jew, love not to
> decorate the temple; though it would be doing
> them an injustice not to observe, that they love to
> attend it. Matters are so managed here, that the
> manse is like the church. After a thaw or a smart
> shower of rain, the inside walls and timber
> exhibit a scene wonderfully striking. The pearly
> drops meet the eye from every point of view; so
> that, among the rigours of winter, its inhabitants

enjoy some of the pleasures of a May morning.
The situation of the manse accounts for this. It
lies in a swamp.'

The minister from Heriot in the Lothians is similarly
somewhat disenchanted with his lot: (II, 271)

'The church is an old and infirm building. It is
scarcely safe to perform public duty in it. It is
neither dry above, nor decently seated. It is,
perhaps, the most shabby and miserable place of
accommodation for divine service in Scotland.'

It is noteworthy from numerous accounts that the
ministers were by no means afraid of speaking out against
the landowners ('heritors'), who were after all their own
patrons, and whose fault it was if buildings were in poor
condition. Complaints against them were various; they are
often blamed, for example, for setting a bad example by
failing to attend church, but sometimes too for the way they
treat their tenants. Here is a particularly outspoken comment
from the pen of the writer for Towie in Aberdeenshire: (XIV,
740)

'A generous mind will never think without
indignation on the desire which many proprietors
of land in this Highland part of the country, have
to keep their tenants in a state of slavish
dependence. That the latter should presume to
think for themselves, and the former have no
other coercion but what reason and the laws of

the country allow them, is a sentiment so little
realised by the lairds, that a poor tenant, if he is
disposed to cringe, will often be preferred to one
whose spirit and circumstances lead him to think
of a manly independence.'

Similarly, some of the ministers are prepared to take up
the cudgels in defence of the schoolmasters, whose lot at
the time was often abysmal. Their salaries had been set
around 100 years before in the reign of William and Mary,
when an Act had been passed to ensure that every parish
should have a school and schoolmaster. What had then been
a reasonable salary was now woefully inadequate, so that
most of the dominies lived in what was described as 'a kind
of genteel starving'. Here is a typical protest, again from Heriot
in the Lothians: (II, 272)

'He [the dominie] is also precentor, gravedigger,
beadle, session-clerk, and yet his whole income
does not exceed £8 sterling. This, with the paltry
accommodation, holds out little encouragement
to a teacher of any merit. Indeed, no man who
possesses strength to lift a mattock or to wield a
flail, would accept of such a disgraceful pittance.'

And the writer from Craignish in Argyll makes his feelings
plain in a similar tone: (VIII, 79)

'The school salary is only 100 merks, and 50s.
arising out of a mortification, which, along with
perquisites, may amount to £20 per annum; a

miserable allowance for a man of genius for employing his time and talents in qualifying the rising generation to fill up the vacant situations in society with honour. What a reproach to the people of Scotland, that this most useful class of citizens, on their late attempt for a small augmentation of salary, could not find, among all those who received the early benefit of their instruction, one to support their honest cause! At this rate, the age of darkness will again commence; and Scotland will, ere long, be as remarkable for wealth and ignorance, as it formerly was for poverty and learning.'

Few of the writers are as passionate as this one, yet again and again complaints are made about the poverty in which these men of learning were forced to live. 'Had not the present teacher been disabled for working as a common mason', comments the minister from Kirkpatrick-Justa in Dumfries-shire, 'he must have spurned such a livelihood as this.' (IV, 341) (Interestingly, the earnings of masons were considerably better; their wages are given in several accounts as anything between 1s. and 1s.8d. per day).

The ministers' ire is also directed against the landlords on account of the short leases granted to their tenants. Again a particularly outspoken comment, this one from the minister of Kirkmichael in Perthshire, will serve as illustration: (XII, 678)

'Few of the tenants enjoy long leases of their

> farms. Holding their small possessions by a small
> and uncertain tenure, they are continually in a
> state of abject dependence on their landlords. Is it
> that landlords are apprehensive of obtaining no
> benefit to themselves from granting leases, or of
> their tenants not having money or skill, or
> industry, for making improvements?'

Many others make the point that the very short leases remove all incentive for making improvements, and that this is one of the factors responsible for the woeful state of agriculture in the country at the time. Another grievance aired by several writers is the quasi-feudal state of affairs prevailing in some parishes; tenants could at times be prevented from attending to their own smallholdings because of the services required of them by their masters.

'Many services, the sad marks of slavery, are demanded', is the bold assertion of the Orkney account for Bressay, Burra and Quarf: (XIX, 394)

> 'They must fish for their masters, who either give
> them a fee entirely inadequate to their labour or
> their dangers, or take their fish at a lower price
> than others would give. It is true, that in years of
> scarcity, they must depend on their landlords for
> the means of subsistence, and are often deep in
> their debt. But why not allow them to make the
> best of their situation? Why not let them have
> leases on reasonable terms, and dispose of their
> produce to those who will give them the best

price? Why not let them fish for themselves? Why
should the laird have any claim except for the
stipulated rent?'

Bold statements of this sort surely provide in themselves
a very real justification of Sir John Sinclair's declared aim of
improving the lot of the poorer folk. It is difficult to imagine
a more effective medium for upholding the rights of the many
who were living under rank injustice at the time.

'Rhubarb, to the value of £160 sterling, was sold in one season to a
London druggist, at the rate of 8s. the pound'

CHAPTER 7

Initiatives

I T IS probably true to say that in every age the temptation exists to look with some condescension on the achievements of an earlier generation. This may be especially true today, as we compare our relatively affluent lifestyle, with its high standards of comfort and technology, with that of our eighteenth century forebears.

Such an attitude, however, receives an immediate check when we are confronted with some of the outstanding examples offered by the writers of the Old Statistical Account. We cannot but respect and admire – and indeed be amazed by – the technical feats of men of undoubted genius, carried out with minimal technical resources.

In this chapter we shall be looking briefly at just a small selection of initiatives, covering a broad spectrum from advances in agriculture and industry to the mammoth operation of clearing the great swamps on the edge of Scotland's central belt.

One disappointing aspect should first be pointed out, which is that again and again the writers make it clear that inventors and innovators are not only undervalued but actually ridiculed, at least in the early stages. Later, when their neighbours have finally seen proof of the advantages of the new system, they may gradually be won over. But it has to be admitted that this negative aspect of the Scots character (arguably still extant in the 'I kent his faither' attitude) comes across in a great many instances.

Consider for example the story of the invention of the threshing-mill by a man of outstanding skill, who clearly had to endure a degree of discouragement which would have daunted a lesser mortal. (XII, 522) 'This is one of the most ingenious and useful inventions that has, perhaps, ever appeared in the world', asserts the minister of Kilmadock and Doune:

> 'The first inventor was Michael Stirling, farmer in Craighead, in the parish of Dunblane, who died in the 89th year of his age, 1796. This venerable old man, when in the prime of life, had a strong propensity to every curious invention; and, after much thought and study, he prepared and finished a machine for threshing his corn in the year 1748, having employed tradesmen to execute the work under his direction. Mr Stirling's ignorant neighbours were, however, no way struck with his invention, but laughed at it, and called him 'a maggotty fellow'. In short, like Noah with his ark, poor Mr Stirling was surrounded only with mockers, and at length concealed his operations altogether. The wonderful powers of the machine, however, soon drew the attention of strangers, who came and picked up models, and so were enabled to

erect others, both in Scotland and England. Mr
Stirling's machine, in one short winter's day,
threshed 50 threaves of stiff outfield corn,
yielding 16 bolls of oats, which would have taken
16 days of one man to thresh with the flail.'

One invention of truly immense importance was that of
a light, efficient chain-plough (later replaced by a swing-
plough), by James Small of Berwickshire in 1765. The
improvement this brought can scarcely be exaggerated.
Description of the older type of ploughs in use come from
every area of the country, depicting almost unbelievably
cumbersome, antiquated implements which required in most
instances several attendants, with anything up to eight or
ten horses or oxen, and with the ploughman often walking
backwards! Here is the comment of the writer for Borthwick
in Berwickshire: (II, 72)

'One ingenious mechanick, indeed, we must not
omit to mention. At the village of Ford lives
James Small, the best plough-maker in Scotland.
In this particular department, indeed, he is
perhaps second to none in the island. He makes
300, 400, and sometimes 500 ploughs in a year,
and by his acknowledged and decided
superiority, such is the demand, he might make
his own terms, and increase the sale of his
ploughs to an incredible extent. His chain plough
is now in general use, and well-known.'

Out of numerous eulogies of pioneers in improving land – something which could scarcely have been more urgently needed – it has been necessary to choose only a few outstanding examples, which will serve to show that inventors were not the only ones to suffer from a lack of appreciation of their efforts. The vital difference made by a good landlord to the wellbeing of the ordinary people is aptly illustrated by the following extract from the report for Tyrie in Aberdeenshire: (XV, 544)

> 'About 40 years ago, a great part of the lands in
> this parish lay in their natural uncultivated state,
> and such of them as were in culture produced
> poor starved crops. What has been done for
> promoting the industry, prosperity, and happiness
> of this parish and neighbourhood, must reflect
> great honour to the memory of the late Alex
> Fraser of Strichen. He first introduced
> improvements; gave lime to his tenants, gratis,
> and, in spite of their prejudices, prevailed with
> them to use it as manure; brought skilful men
> from the south country, who taught them how to
> sow grass seeds, and raise turnips, cabbage and
> potatoes in the fields. He gave them leases during
> their lives, at a reasonable rate; and did not think
> his interests hurt when he saw his tenants
> enjoying the comforts of life; nor did he treat
> them like cattle, as occasions offered. The good
> effect of these encouragements are, extensive

fields regularly laid out, fine stone fences, good
houses built with stone and lime, excellent crops
of turnips, sown grass, and almost all sorts of
grain, stocks of cattle, full corn yards, and
everywhere the appearance of plenty; and all
ranks of people are more industrious and more
healthy than formerly.'

Sadly, this was far from being the norm. Most still lived
in dire poverty. And while bad landlords were undoubtedly
to blame in some cases, it has to be said that equal blame
attached to the stubborn prejudices of the people themselves.
Once again the sheer diversity of the reports can be seen in
this excerpt from the parish of Leslie in Aberdeenshire, not
far from the one above where the people's lot had so
improved: (XV, 267)

'Though instances of improvement daily occur,
and the benefits resulting from thence are
obvious, an obstinate attachment to old
established procedures too much prevails, and
neither precept nor example will induce them to
alter their plan.'

One item of unusual interest in the agricultural accounts
has to do with the eradication of a particularly noxious weed,
known as gool – a kind of wild chrysanthemum. The writer
of the report for Cargill in Perthshire explains: (XI, 59)

'An old custom takes place in this parish, known
as gool-riding, which seems worthy of

observation. The lands of Cargill were formerly so very much over-run by a weed with a yellow flower which grows among the corns, especially in wet seasons, called gool, and which had the most pernicious effects, not only upon the corn while growing, but also in preventing their winning after being cut down, that it was found absolutely necessary to adopt some effectual method of extirpating it altogether. Accordingly, after allowing a reasonable time for procuring clean seed from other quarters, an act of baron-court was passed, enforcing an old Act of Parliament to the same effect, in posing a fine of 3s. 4d. or a wedder sheep, on the tenants, for every stock of gool that should be found growing among their corns on a particular day; and certain persons called gool-riders, were appointed to ride through the field, search for gool, and carry the law into execution when they discovered it. Though the fine of a wedder sheep is now commuted and reduced to 2d. sterling, for every stock of gool, the practice of gool-riding is still kept up, and the fine rigidly exacted. The effects of the baronial regulation have been salutary beyond what could well have been expected. Five stocks of gool were formerly said to grow for every stock of corn through all the lands of the barony, and 20 threaves of barley did not then produce one boll. Now the grounds are so

cleared of this noxious weed, that the corns are
in high demand for seed; and after the most
diligent search, the gool-riders can hardly
discover as many growing stock of gool, the fine
for which will afford them a dinner and a drink.'

Another story of agricultural improvement comes from
one of the Orkney accounts, from the parish of Shapinsay,
where a spirited new owner had clearly transformed his land:
(XIX, 280)

'Previous to his purchase, nothing was to be seen
over its whole extent but a dreary waste,
interspersed with lands ill-cultivated, a few
miserable hovels thinly scattered over its surface,
which were not fit to shelter from the rigours of the
climate a few ragged inhabitants, dirty through
indolence, lean with hunger, or torpid by despair.

'Everything on this estate now happily wears a
very different and more pleasant aspect. An
elegant house has been built, and an extensive
garden laid out; the lands substantially inclosed,
and judiciously cultivated with the English plough;
many barren fields are, by cultivation, made fertile;
summer fallowing, with a change of seed and
rotation of crops, is introduced with good effect;
and the soil, which formerly bore with reluctance
coarse grass and scanty heather, and puny oats
and bear, now cheerfully produces oats, rye,

barley, pease, wheat, potatoes, clover, and turnips, in considerable quantity and of a good quality.

'Together with these improvements, the same gentleman has erected a little village by the side of the harbour of Elwick, in which he has placed joiners, carpenters, weavers, tailors, shoemakers, coopers, and labourers of various sorts, furnished them with work sufficient to employ them; and thus enabled them from the fruits of their industry to marry early, and to produce numerous families.'

Potatoes had, during the eighteenth century, become a very important part of the ordinary people's diet, and many of the reports pay tribute not only to the worth of this root but also to those agricultural improvers who pioneered their cultivation. Here is one example, from Kilsyth: (IX, 475)

'If the name of any man deserves to be handed down to succeeding ages with honour and gratitude, it is that of Robert Graham Esq., of Tamrawer. He, with a spirit truly patriotic, and a mind active and indefatigable, set vigorously to work in the cultivation of potatoes, in the year 1739. Had they [the people] known the amazing benefit that was to accrue to the nation from his fortunate attempt, they would have doubtless hailed the auspicious event, and erected a monument to Mr Graham, on the spot. He raised the cultivation of potatoes in the neighbourhood

of Kilsyth to a pitch scarcely yet, if at all,
surpassed anywhere.'

From these and similar eulogies there emerges a sad picture of what rural Scotland was like before the improvers began the work of transformation – of land largely undrained and unfertilised, often choked with weeds; of crop rotations and planting dates firmly fixed by tradition, with most attempts at innovation met with deep suspicion or downright antagonism; of cumbersome, antiquated implements and malnourished livestock. But a gradual awakening had begun, led by enlightened proprietors, gentlemen farmers and often also the parish ministers. The happy result was that in at least some areas, crop yields had greatly increased and the wellbeing of the poorer folk had at last begun to improve. They were even finding themselves with a little cash to spend.

Turning to animal husbandry, one finds in certain cases a surprisingly modern attitude. Here, for example, is the record of a breeding experiment – which is even controlled! The writer for the parish of Twyneholme and Kirk-Christ in the Borders describes it thus: (V, 357)

'A gentleman in this country, who had a large dairy,
remarkable for rearing the best cattle, and who
kept and fed them till the proper age, when he sent
them with other cattle which he bought from his
tenants, to the English market, to try an
experiment bought one of Mr Bakewell's bulls. He
put the half of his own cows to this, and the other
half to a Moorland bull, bred upon his own estate.

He fed the product equally, till they were sent to
market in Norfolk, when those bred from the
Galloway bull brought considerably more money
that the others, besides being easier to feed.'

From the account for Strathblane in Stirlingshire comes
mention of another experiment, again demonstrating a grasp
of the modern concept of controlled trial. The normal practice
in protecting sheep from parasites was to smear their coats
with a mixture of butter and tar. Here, though, a local farmer
took 100 lambs of the same stock and divided them equally,
smearing fifty and leaving fifty unsmeared. At sheep-shearing,
he found it took seven unsmeared fleeces to weigh one stone,
whereas it took only four of those smeared. Continuing his
research for five more years, he carried out tests to reduce
the cost of smearing, and found that 'two pints of buttermilk
mixed with six Scotch pints of tar would smear four more
than tar and butter alone'. We may be inclined to smile at all
of this. But it surely demonstrates a spirit of enquiry and
enterprise ahead of its time.

The Dunkeld account includes a reference to an interesting – and highly lucrative – experiment carried out in the
garden of the Duke of Atholl, on the growing of rhubarb.
Although this would later be found in every cottage garden,
it was at that time a rare plant much prized for its aperient
qualities: (XII, 343)

'In 1770, some seeds of the true rheum
palmatum were sent from Petersburgh by Dr
Mounsey to His Grace. They were planted, and

considerable attention was paid to the culture of
that root. Rhubarb, to the value of £160 sterling,
was sold in one season to a London druggist, at
the rate of 8s. the pound. In short, full proof was
afforded, that rhubarb may be raised in Britain,
equal in all its qualities to what is now, at so high
a price, imported from the East Indies, and from
Russia and Turkey.'

Before we leave the subject of agriculture it may be of
interest to note reference to what might well have been the
first ploughing match in Scotland at Alloa: (IX, 669)

'Just as the spirit of improvement was beginning
to shew itself, an intelligent East Lothian farmer
took a farm in this parish, who was remarkable
for his good plowing, draining, and dressing of
his grounds. His example quickened the diligence
of his neighbours. A few years after he was
settled here, he proposed to his landlord and
brother farmers to have trials of skill among the
ploughmen; which scheme was eagerly adopted,
and PLOWING MATCHES were first established,
in 1784. Last spring (1791), 40 ploughs
appeared. The improved chain plough, on Small's
construction, was the only one used. To any one
fond of husbandry, the sight was most
uncommonly delightful and pleasing.'

Not only so, but what an immense amount of enjoyment, not to mention continuity of valuable skills, has been generated ever since by ploughing matches in every area.

Turning attention to industrial development, we find a great many references to the weaving of linen. Apart from agriculture, this was in fact Scotland's chief industry for much of the eighteenth century. It is perhaps of particular interest to learn something of how it began, so that this excerpt from the Morayshire parish of Cullen is worth quoting in full: (XVI, 123)

> 'Before the year 1748, the inhabitants of Cullen were as poor and idle as any set of people in the north. There was no industry, trade, nor manufacturing among them; their only employment was to labour a few acres of land, and to keep tippling-houses; and often to drink with one another, to consume the beer for want of customers.

> 'The late Earl of Findlater, that true patriot, pitying the situation of the people, resolved to introduce the linen manufacture among them. And here, perhaps, it may not be improper to mention the method he adopted to promote this purpose. He brought two or three gentlemen's sons from Edinburgh, who had been regularly bred there to the business, and who had some patrimony of their own; but to their encouragement to settle so far north, he gave each £600 free of interest for seven years; after which, the money was to be

repaid by £50 yearly, the remainder in their hands to be always free of interest.

'Besides this, he built excellent weaving shops, and furnished every accommodation at very reasonable prices. So good a plan, and so great encouragement, could not fail of success. In a few years, the manufacture was established to the extent desired. All the young people were engaged in the business, and even the old found employment in various ways by the manufactures; and thus a spirit of industry was diffused over the place and neighbourhood in a very short time, which soon appeared in their comfortable mode of living, and their dress.'

This was of course industry on a fairly small scale, but the improvement to the lifestyle of the poor is very obvious. And indeed, even in some Highland glens there are to be found examples of linen weaving being encouraged by benevolent proprietors, with the same benefits following. In Glenurquhart near Inverness, for example, Sir James Grant had a lint mill built for the people: (XVIII, 260)

'As a result, industry has been encouraged among the females, and both sexes exhibit, on Sundays and holy-days, a much improved appearance from what they were wont to do formerly, by being dressed in linen of their own growth and manufacture.'

At the same time, capitalists were setting up cotton mills all over Scotland; but this was by no means on a small scale. In the New Lanark mill established by David Dale in 1786, for instance, there were 1,334 workers aged from six years upwards, who toiled from six in the morning until seven at night. These children had an hour and a half off for meals, and then went to school until nine. And this was widely acclaimed as an enlightened regime! Admittedly it was superior to many others – for example, in that the owner took an interest in the children's diet.

It is in their attitude to the cotton industry with its huge numbers of workers that we find most divergence in the ministers' views. To some, any industry is considered a great benefit; to others, it bodes ill both for morals and health. An example of each of these views follows.

From the account for Auchtergaven in Perthshire of the Stanley cotton works: (XII, 34)

> 'Near a hundred families now reside in the village
> of Stanley. Above 350 persons are employed
> about the cotton mill – of this number, 300 are
> women or children under 16 years of age. The
> boys and girls, although confined at work in the
> mill for many hours of the day, and at times
> during the night, are, in general, very healthy.'

This rosy view is by no means shared by the writer of the Paisley account: (VII, 827)

> 'The numbers that are brought together, the

confinement, the breathing of an air loaded with the dust and downy particles of the cotton, and contaminated with the effluvia of rancid oil arising from the machinery, must prove hurtful in a high degree to the delicate lungs of the children.'

Another who has grave doubts, the writer for Fintry in Stirlingshire, has this to say: (IX, 335)

'Notwithstanding present opinions, it still remains in doubt, whether this revolution in the state of a country, will in the end prove a national advantage. Whether a pallid and sickly race, brought up in the confined air of cotton mills, with few attachments, and little education, will compensate for the sturdy sons of our hills and mountains, or afford a set of as loyal and virtuous subjects, is a question we leave posterity to answer.'

One very different industry which had been carried out over a long period was logging, descriptions of which in the accounts make intriguing reading. Here is one from the account for Speymouth: (XVI, 668)

'At Garmouth, or at the mouth of Spey, there is a wood trade, the most considerable, it is supposed, of any in Scotland, for home wood. The wood is mostly fir, with some little oak and birch. It comes from the extensive forests in Strathspey and Badenoch, and is floated down the River Spey in deals, planks, logs and spars. . . The wood is

> partly sold at Garmouth, to the people of the
> adjacent country by two men, at the rate of 30s.
> per raft. The logs and spars are, for the most part,
> floated down the river loose, to the number of,
> perhaps, 20,000 pieces at a time, with men going
> along the side of the river with long poles, to push
> them on, as they stick on the banks. These men
> have 1s. 2d. per day, besides whisky; and there
> will sometimes be from 50 to 80 employed at
> once in the floating.'

One example of enterprise which challenges us today, with environmental issues firmly on the agenda, is the extent to which even small rivers were used as a source of hydro power. Often reference is made to a single river having several mills within quite a short distance – as here in the account for the parish of Mains in Angus: (XIII, 487)

> 'Dighty, the only river in the parish, drives more
> machinery for its size than, perhaps, any water in
> Britain; every fall upon it turns a mill; so that
> within this parish, though not above four miles in
> length, there are no fewer than 33 mills erected
> for different purposes. There are several corn
> mills, barley mills, and mills for washing and
> cleaning yarn. There are also upon the water of
> Dighty, a waulk mill and a snuff mill.'
> [Note: The Scots dictionary defines waulking as
> 'a process to make cloth thick and felted by
> soaking, beating and shrinking'].

This record seems to be eclipsed, however, by the list offered in the Collington, Edinburgh, report (although, to be fair, this was an urban location): (II, 140)

'This small river does more work than any other, even of the largest size in Scotland. In the course of about ten miles it drives the following mills:

corn mills	14
barley mills	12
flour mills	20
lint mills	2
waulk mills	5
paper mills	4
snuff mills	5
leather mills	2
saw mills	7
TOTAL	71'

Perhaps, after all, this could be considered a draw? The Angus example has 33 mills in four miles; the Edinburgh one 71 in ten! For both, undoubtedly, an amazing total.

All of the foregoing initiatives, whether in agriculture or industry, should serve to demonstrate the lively spirit of enterprise of which late eighteenth century Scots were capable, although at the same time, sadly, it has to be remembered that despite these improvements, the majority of the poor were still living in a manner not far removed from that of mediaeval times.

One immense achievement has been left to the end, one which dwarfs all others, and that is the mammoth task by which the great swamps on the edge of Scotland's Central Belt were cleared.

In the earlier part if the century this whole area was still a vast, impenetrable bog, stretching approximately from Stirling to Aberfoyle. In three of the accounts, a description is offered of the reclamation of this area and its transformation into prime agricultural land. It makes fascinating reading.

In this context it is impossible to offer a detailed picture of the whole massive operation – e.g. the methods of clearing used; the composition of the moss (in which, interestingly, not a single pebble was found, only shells left by the retreat of the sea); the dealings with the labour force, and their exploitation by certain of the landlords; and the gradual improvement of their lot – all of this is dealt with in the reports. But it is certainly well worth reading, and is to be found in Vol.XII, pp. 574-604. Here only a brief summary is given.

Various attempts had been made earlier to clear parts of the moss. One landowner, for instance, had planted trees which he later claimed to be thriving, despite the four feet of moss in which they grew! Others had tried to plough the moss, and had set fire to it when it was dry, 'incorporating the ashes with the remaining bog-earth to produce a coarse grass'.

All such attempts were abandoned, however, when the revolutionary method conceived by Lord Kames, owner of the Drummond estates, was put into operation. He had conducted experiments to show that the moss could be carried off by a powerful stream of water (eventually ejected by a large pumping wheel), to leave behind the potentially fertile clay underneath.

One thing was necessary for success – to find a labour force willing not only to carry out the back-breaking task of throwing a huge mass of moss into the specially-dug drains at high speed, but also to endure being drenched and cold all day long. Found they were, though – and it is a poignant story – in poverty-stricken Highlanders who had been dis-possessed in favour of sheep in some of the earlier clearances.

Their lot was hard. Living at first in rude huts which are said to have actually floated on the morass, they were held in derision by the local folk, who called them 'moss lairds', and further isolated by their speaking only Gaelic. The terms of their employment by some (but not all) of the landowners involved what can only be described as gross exploitation.

As the years went by their conditions did improve. A specially-qualified bilingual teacher was supplied; gradually they seem to have been integrated into the community. Of those changed days the minister writes:

> 'The moss settlers comprise 764 men, women and children, with 54 carts, 201 cows, and 102 brick houses.'

Leaving aside the undoubtedly outstanding achievement commemorated in the Old Statistical Account, it seems rather fitting to finish this chapter with a testimonial to the labourers instead. They were, the minister asserts:

> 'A sober, frugal and industrious people. Neither
> ought it to be forgotten that, from their settlement
> to this present day, not a single instance has
> occurred among them of theft, bad
> neighbourhood, or of any other misdemeanour,
> that required the interposition of the civil
> magistrate. Nor, however poor the
> circumstances, has any one of them ever
> stooped to solicit assistance from the parish
> funds appropriated to that purpose.'

So when we drive through that area of fertile agricultural countryside today in our fast cars, perhaps we might spare a thought, not only in gratitude for the absence of the great bog, but also for the honourable folk who toiled there, soaked to the skin, more than two hundred years ago.

'. . . it is painful to observe, that what should be a support to their future families, and a provision for sickness and old age, is misapplied in the purchase of silks, laces, lawns and tinsel!'

CHAPTER 8

Outspoken Comments

I T SEEMS appropriate at this point to stop and reflect imaginatively on what it must have meant for a parish minister, in that final decade of the eighteenth century, to receive one of Sir John Sinclair's questionnaires.

Surely it cannot have been anything but extremely daunting! Not only was he faced with 166 questions, but each branch, so to speak, is found to sprout several twigs. One cannot be sure just how busy these learned men would have been – no doubt the workload varied from parish to parish – but even to record all the answers after all the 'statistics' had been collected, and to add lengthy comments, using a quill pen and ink, must have been no mean task. At one stage too Sir John actually lost 12 accounts! One can only hope that the unfortunate writers had kept copies, but it is unlikely.

Four sample questions have been selected as illustrations:

> Q. 19 about fish:
> What sorts of fish are caught on the coast? In
> what quantity? At what prices sold? How taken?
> And to what market sent?

Q. 103 about livestock:
What at an average is supposed to be the number
of cattle, sheep, horses, and goats, in the district?

Q. 146 about history:
Are there any Roman, Saxon, Danish, or Pictish
castles, camps, altars, roads, forts, or other
remains of antiquity? And what traditions of
historical accounts are there of them?

Q. 154 about industry:
Are the people disposed to industry? What
manufactures are carried on in the parish? And
what number of hands are employed therein?

The sheer hard work involved in this research can readily
be understood. Assessing the numbers of livestock alone
must have been a challenge – help would obviously be
required for this – but it is worth pointing out that the numbers
of animals involved were considerable. For example, in one
small area of Highland Perthshire alone, the totals given are
11,000 cattle, 70,000 sheep, 3,500 horses. Small wonder
that the ministers often referred to livestock as being under-
sized and at times half-starved.

Not surprisingly, the writers often ignored numerous
questions altogether, although it should be added that some
wrote outstandingly and at length. Many tended to major on
their own pet subjects, for example, archaeology, place-
names, botany or wildlife. Others used the opportunity to

speak out against injustice, a good example being the exploitation of the dominies. Unpopular taxes, the Salt Tax and the Coal Tax, also found a prominent place in some reports.

The bulk of the material in the entire Old Statistical Account, however, centres on agriculture. Many wrote with such impressive knowledge, and demonstrating such profound interest, that one couldn't help wondering how much time they gave to their human flocks! One, the Rev. Robert Rennie of Kilsyth, was even invited by the Tsar of Russia to become professor of agriculture at St Petersburg University – an offer he declined. The minister of Doune in Perthshire, clearly another enthusiast, devotes no fewer than 18 pages to agriculture, under the following headings: draining, levelling, stone-clearing, trenching, straightening marches and burns, dividing runrig lands and commons, inclosing, crop rotations, size of farms, leases and rents, implements of husbandry, threshing-mills, sales of grain, agricultural wages, black cattle, horses, sheep, markets, and price of provisions.

A great many others display a keen interest in such matters. And because the Old Statistical Account records a period of transition, making it very clear that an 'agricultural revolution' emphatically does not happen overnight, nor does it mean steady, uniform changes happening all over the country, it is not surprising that some of the writers' comments express their frustration over lack of forward movement in their own parishes.

Here are a few of the more outspoken comments on the agricultural scene:

On crop rotations: (Wamphray, Borders, IV, 351)

'I almost blush to mention these. A favoured
piece of land has a great deal of indulgence
shown it when it is put under the following, viz.
after manure, three crops of oats; dung, and
drilled potatoes; nay, twice or thrice cut, and two
or three years' pasture.'

(Glasford, Lanarkshire, VII, 22276)
'The spirit of improvement has not yet reached
this parish. There is in it only one man who
deserves the name of farmer. To improve land
requires both industry and skill. Few of the
farmers here have even a moderate portion of
either, and many are defective in both.'

(Birse, Aberdeenshire, XIV, 417)
'Some are going on with spirit, inclosing and
clearing their ground of stones. Others are
throwing every impediment in the way of the
improver, by trampling down the fences, and by
not only neglecting to remove the stones from
their fields, but even by alleging that the stones are
beneficial to the soil, and tend to nourish the crop.'

One who sees the less acceptable side of the improvements: (Auchtertoul, Fife, X, 66)

'This taste for enlarging and uniting farms, which

seems to be on the increase throughout Scotland, will perhaps eventually be unfavourable to the population of the country, and most undoubtedly, to the character and morals of the inhabitants. It forces the people from the active, healthy employments of a country life, to take refuge in manufacturing towns and populous cities, which may be said to be the graves of human spirits.'

Clearly many of the ministers regarded the landowners' reluctance to allow their tenants leases of reasonable length as a bar to progress of any sort, and were unafraid to voice their views, as the following excerpts show:

(Mortlach, Banff, XVI, 329)
'Agriculture is on the improving hand; but short leases are the bane of every improvement. Who in his senses would make a farm more valuable, at his own dear expense, only to induce another to covet and bid for it?'

(Buittle, Borders, V, 218)
'It is probable that leases longer than those of 19 years [the general length at the time] would be favourable to permanent improvements, such as hedges, and it must be owned that as the lease draws near its close, the tenant is often found comporting himself, as if under a conviction that he inhabited hostile ground. To say the truth, that narrowness of mind, or aristocratical pride, which

adjusted every manner of lease to the visible
purpose of keeping tenants in abject subjection
upon their landlords, has of late been put very
much to the blush.'

(Killearnan, Ross, XVII, 418)
'The agricultural state of this parish will further be
accounted for, when it is mentioned that leases
are, with very few exceptions, unknown. The
farms on the most considerable property have
been let only from year to year. . . What
inducement does this present for improvement?'

Passing on to comments about the management of livestock, we find in some places a distressing lack of care for
their welfare which the writers are not slow to expose:
(Barvas, Lewis, XX, 5)

'All the sheep, except a few of the black-faced
kind introduced by the minister, are remarkably
small. Though very wild, they are in general so
far tame, that they can be driven into small
inclosures, where the wool is pulled off, a
barbarous custom which certainly must be
detrimental to the animal and its wool, and
indeed proves fatal when the weather happens to
be severe immediately after plucking.'

(Shapinsay, Orkney, XIX, 275)
'Instead of their being directed by the tender

attentive care of a shepherd, sheep are attacked with sticks and stones [when they encroach upon farmland] and hunted by dogs, with more fury than is commonly used to ravenous beasts in other countries. Hence these animals, which under proper management might be a source of wealth to the proprietor, and a benefit to the country at large, are decreasing in number, and degenerating in quality so fast, that in a short time, if the mode of treatment is not altered, they will not be worth the raising.'

(Hoy and Graemsay, Orkney, XIX, 108)
'The sheep run wild in these mountains, and are never got until they run them down with their dogs and by that means they are much abused. Some of these sheep will run with more than three of four years' wool on them, and when hounded by their dogs, they run generally to the rocks, where there is no possibility of access to them. Many of their young lambs are devoured, and picked up by eagles and other birds of prey.'

The writer of the Gigha account is deeply concerned about a certain cruel practice in his area – and one which sadly was also more widespread: (XX, 424)

'A practice is sometimes used, though not so common as in other places, of tying the harrow to the horse's tail. This is often done to save the

expense and trouble of a harness, and
sometimes to tame young horses, as they term it,
which indeed, it does with a vengeance. For the
honour of human nature, as well as from a regard
to the safety and ease of that noble animal, to
which we are indebted for a great share of the
pleasures and conveniences of life, it were to be
wished that other proprietors would form a
resolution, to put an effective stop to such cruelty.
'A merciful man hath compassion on his beast'.'

To end this selection of outspoken comments on the
general state of agriculture, here are two written by ministers
who clearly do not fear the reaction of their parishioners at a
later date:

(Avoch, Ross-shire, XVII, 305)
'Among the farmers here, farming is only in a
state of infancy. It has emerged but little from the
rude practice of their forefathers, 100 years ago.'

(Banchory Tarnan, XIV, 305)
'The state of agriculture is, in general, much the
same as it has been in the memory of man.'

And to illustrate just how greatly the scene varied from
parish to parish, and how altogether piecemeal was this
'revolution' in agriculture during the 1790s, we find a contrast-
ingly upbeat report from Kirriemuir in Angus: (XIII, 358)

'What is wet, they are draining; what is

uncultivated and arable, they are bringing into
tillage; what is not arable, they are planting.'

It may not seem surprising that the ministers frequently
vented their ire on the 'heritors' on account of the dilapidated
(and at times almost ruinous) state of their churches and
manses – until one remembers that it was on these landowners that their own livelihoods depended! Many are very
outspoken indeed, as in this report from one of the Orkney
parishes of Hoy & Graemsay: (XIX, 109)

> 'The whole of the church about nine years ago
> fell down of itself before the heritors would offer
> to make any reparation on it; at last they rebuilt it,
> and that in a very slight manner, so that it is not
> above half-finished. The manse is in a very
> ruinous condition, although built since the
> incumbency of this present minister, and that of
> the very worst materials that could possibly be
> got, so that it is now dangerous to walk upon the
> floors, as the whole of them are worm-eaten.'

This comment from Halkirk in Caithness demonstrates
a similarly unsatisfactory situation: (XVIII, 92)

> 'The manse and church, during the present
> incumbency, have always been in a bad state of
> repair, although repaired four times. It is to be
> regretted that heritors, from a mistaken notion of
> saving their purses, should so unaccountably
> injure their own interest, and incommode the

minister, when both might have been avoided
with small expense.'

But decaying churches and manses were not to be found
only in the far north, as this excerpt shows: (Heriot, Lothians,
II, 347)

'This church is an old and infirm building. It is
scarcely safe to perform public duty in it. It is
neither dry above, nor decently seated. It is,
perhaps, the most shabby and miserable place of
accommodation for divine service in Scotland.'

Some of the ministers are not above taking a swipe at
the 'dissenters' in their parishes; others are more benign in
their comments. While an overwhelming majority in most
places adhered to the national Church, there were – notably
in the central belt – various breakaway groups; although no
longer persecuted for their beliefs, they were still regarded
with suspicion, or active dislike at times, by both their fellow
citizens and by some ministers. One understandable cause
of annoyance was their failure to contribute to poor relief
(normally provided by church collections, use of the mort-
cloth to cover the coffin at funerals, and interest on certain
bequests).

The minster of Kilchattan and Killbrandon in Argyll is no
great admirer of the dissenters in his own parish: (VIII, 181)

'There are no sectaries except a few, whose charity
is not very extensive. Charity with them is confined
to the household of faith, the members of which

they are at no loss to distinguish, and evidently find
them to be few.'

A similarly critical opinion comes from the Angus parish
of Rescobie: (XIII, 591)

'It might be reckoned an illiberal attack on
weakness were any attempt made to expose their
errors; nor is this the place. But let it not offend
them, if it be observed, that their distinguishing
marks are not very ornamental, nor their proper
peculiarities extremely praiseworthy.'

The great majority of Scotland's ministers at the time
belonged to the party known as 'Moderates'. They tended to
focus strongly on morality rather than doctrine, comfortable
with parishioners who were law-abiding and respectable,
and surprisingly scornful of evangelistic zeal. The terms
'sober and industrious' and 'peaceable and contented' occur
repeatedly in the reports, while 'enthusiasm' is a derogatory
word used to describe parishioners who display religious
fervour. The following description of a religious revival by
the minister of Kilsyth – doubtless in the face of strong
scepticism – must therefore rank as a fairly outspoken
comment. Although this movement had taken place some
fifty years earlier, he maintains that its influence continues:
(IX, 444)

'If strife and contention, wrath and malice
ceased, and love and peace and forbearance, and
long-suffering and forgivenss of one another,

> prevailed; if the thief stole no more, but made
> restitution; and a whole parish at once, became
> decent and devout, and sober and serious; and
> that they did so, is attested by pastor and
> heritors, elders and magistrates, and by all the
> wise and worthy men of the congregation of
> Kilsyth, who were eyewitnesses of the events,
> and are still alive; call this enthusiasm, or call it
> by any other name, I pray God, that I may ever
> feel its influence, and bear testimony to its power
> among the people.'

Here is a bold attack by a minister on a local laird whose pigeons are feasting on the much-needed food of the poor. It is an important issue; all over Scotland this particular injustice was causing hardship at the time: (Auchterderran, Fife, X, 52)

> 'It has been doubted whether our law authorising
> pigeon-houses is not, in some degree, contrary to
> natural equity, as it does not seem reasonable
> that any one should keep a house furnished with
> a multitude of animals, over which he has no
> government, and which prey on his neighbour's
> corn as freely as on his own, while he alone has
> the profit.'

One thing which excites the ire of the writers almost more than anything else is the dire situation of the schoolmasters. Here is one example of a frank comment. Describing the excellence of the grammar school in the small Morayshire town of Nairn, the writer goes on to add: (XVI, 744)

> 'Gentlemen from all quarters of the country, and some from England, send their children to be educated here. Every branch of education, which now makes such a noise in the academies, is taught at Nairn, in perfection. Several scholars are annually sent to the universities; and many gentlemen, who now make a figure in distant parts of the world, and not a few who are an ornament to their country at home, in the learned professions, received their education at Nairn within these past 25 years, from the present teacher. The salary is only a chalder of victual; and even that paid in pecks and lippies by the tenants. What a pity, that men of abilities and character, who dedicate their time and labours to the improvements of youth, should be so poorly rewarded, as the generality of schoolmasters in Scotland are! It is truly melancholy to think, that grooms and footmen should receive such extravagant wages, while a body of men, on whose labours the welfare of society doth so much depend, should, in a manner, be neglected and overlooked!'

Similarly passionate in his concern over another of the burning issues of the day – replacing people by sheep- is the minister of Lochbroom in Wester Ross: (XVII, 562)

'The oppression of the landholders is a general
complaint in the Highlands; and the consequence
is that great numbers of the people are forced to
emigrate to America, while others go to service in
the low countries [Lowlands] and manufacturing
towns. And thus the population is not near so
great as might be expected in such an extent of
territory. Another circumstance, which is
unfriendly to population, is the engrossing of
farms for sheep-walks. This mode of farming has
been introduced lately into some parts of this
parish, and proved the occasion of reducing to
hardship several honest families, who had lived
tolerably happily on the fruits of their industry
and frugality. Whoever would wish to see the
population of this country flourishing, should do
all in their power to put a stop to the sheep
traffic, and to introduce manufactures among the
people. Whole districts have been already
depopulated by the introduction of sheep; so
that, where formerly hundred of people could be
seen, no human faces are now to be met with,
except a shepherd attended by his dog.'

A note of irony creeps into this equally passionate
statement of opposition to sheep-walks by the Selkirk writer:
(III, 707)

'To restore this country to its former state of
respectability, as well as beauty, it must be

indebted to the proprietors of the soil, for replacing
not only the woods, but the inhabitants, which the
impolitic practice of adding farm to farm, and the
fatal operation of poor-rates, have compelled to
leave their native home. It is painful to see (as in
this parish) one person rent a property, on which
one hundred inhabitants were reared to the state,
and found a comfortable subsistence. It adds to
the bleakness of the scene, to see a few shepherds
strolling over the face of the country, which
formerly was the nurse of heroes, who were justly
accounted the bulwark of their native soil, being
ever ready to brave danger and death in its
defence.'

Protests by the ministers against a perceived 'taste for
luxury' in their parishioners are common in the reports. In
the final decade of the eighteenth century the humbler folk
were at last beginning to find a little extra cash to spend on
clothes; the 'luxury', though, could mean merely a maidservant having the effrontery to wear a silk gown – or even a
ribbon or two – to church. Here is one fairly typical comment,
from the minister of Symington in Ayrshire, who clearly
believed the lower orders should keep their place: (VI, 642)

'They have a taste for dress, and young women
of the middle, and even of the lower ranks,
would now blush to be seen in the blue cloaks,
red plaids, and plain caps, which only twenty
years ago adorned their sex. Nay, even the scarlet

mantle, which lately was a badge of distinction
among the daughters of the farmers, is now
despised; and, O tempora! O mores! the silk-
worms of the East must be pillaged, to deck the
shoulders of our milk-maids.'
(One may at least admire the flamboyance of the
writing!)

Criticism is not confined to the women and girls, as in this
excerpt from the account for Daviot and Dunlichty: (XVII, 63)

'Our young men, how soon they are fit for labour,
go to the south country, or elsewhere, for their
employment; where they remain some part of the
Spring, together with all the summer and harvest.
This practice operates much against improvements
in agriculture, is inimical to the general prosperity
of the people, and productive of these two evils to
the farmer and tenants in particular, viz.
extravagant wages to the few labourers who, from
choice or necessity, may happen to remain at
home; and the introduction of fine clothes, and
other luxuries, among the lower classes.'

To be fair, some writers are clearly concerned that excessive expenditure on dress may well endanger the welfare of
the family, as in this report from Glenorchay & Inishail in
Argyll: (VIII, 124)

'Every man of humanity is pleased to see them
[women] clad in decent and suitable apparel; but it

is painful to observe, that what should be a
support to their future families, and a provision for
sickness and old age, is misapplied in the
purchase of silks, laces, lawns and tinsel! But the
moralist may speculate on this female infirmity as
he chuses; as far as the lass has cash or credit to
procure braws, she will, step by step, follow hard
after what she deems grand in her betters.'

We would expect some interesting comments on whisky-
drinking by the ministers. We are not disappointed! The writer
from the Lothians parish of Bo'ness asserts that public
houses: (II, 703)

'. . . ensnare the innocent, become the haunts of
the idle and dissipated, and ruin annually the
health and morals of thousands of mankind.'

He ends with a quotation from some verses entitled
'Scotland's Skaith' [Scots = harm, hurt].

'O' a' the ills poor Caledonia
E'er yet preed [Scots = tasted], or e'er will taste,
Brewed in hell's black Pandemonia,
Whisky's ill will skaith her maist.'

From the parish of Sorbie comes this similar condemnation: (V, 512)

'The effects of public houses are most injurious
to the morals and industry of the people,
especially when little else than whisky is sold in

> them. A few pence procures as much of this base
> spirit as is sufficient to make any man mad. The
> landlords of superfluous petty public houses
> generally waste their time, and ruin their
> constitutions, by acting like decoys on their silly
> half-resolved neighbours. In their shameless
> business they are flattered with the notion of
> promoting trade.'

A final adverse comment from Callander brings in a note
of genuine concern: (XII, 188)

> 'The number of dram houses is out of all bounds
> too great. These haunts of the idle, of the prodigal
> and profane, contaminate the morals of the lower
> classes of the people beyond description. A poor
> widow must pay a tax before she can obtain a
> candle to give her light, in spinning for the support
> of her fatherless children, and yet a dram-seller, it
> seems, can get a licence, under the sanction of
> law, for little more than one shilling, to corrupt the
> morals of lieges for a whole year.'

'Convulsions were once very common in this parish, especially during
the time of divine service; but are now quite extinct. The cure is
attributed to a rough fellow of a Kirk Officer, who tossed a woman in
that state, with whom he was often plagued, into a ditch full of water.'

CHAPTER 9

Memorable Stories

THERE IS a particular fascination in delving into what is called, prosaically, 'primary source material' – or in plainer language, stories coming straight from the horse's mouth. I feel privileged to be able to peer through a window into the Scotland of the late eighteenth century and to become aware of things which were causing the folk of the time enjoyment, anxiety, sorrow, anger or wonder.

Clearly Sir John Sinclair was looking for remarkable stories when he included the following in his questionnaire:

> Is there any part of the parish subject to inundations or land floods?
> When did any remarkable event of that nature happen?
> Hath there been any remarkable mischief done by thunder and lightning, water spouts or whirlwinds? Have any remarkable phenomena been observed in the air?

A most intriguing response came from the report for Kenmore by Loch Tayside in Perthshire: (XII, 461)

> 'On Sunday the 12th September, about nine o'clock in the morning, an unusual disturbance was observed in Loch Tay, near the village of Kenmore. That village stands at the east end of

the lake, having the river which there issues from the lake, on the north side, and a bay about 460 yards in length and 200 yards in breadth, on the south. The greater part of this bay is very shallow, being generally no more than two or three feet deep. At the extremity of the bay, the water was observed to retire about five yards within its ordinary boundary, and in four or five minutes to flow out again. In this manner it ebbed and flowed successively four or five times in the space of a quarter of an hour, when all at once the water rushed from the east and west in opposite currents towards a lake across the bay, and about the edge of the deep rose in the form of a great wave, to the height of five feet above the ordinary level, leaving the bottom of the bay dry, to the distance of between 80 and 100 yards from its natural boundary. When the opposite currents met, they made a clashing noise, and foamed; and the stronger impulse being from the east, the wave, after rising to its greatest height, rolled westward, but slowly diminishing as it went, for the space of five minutes, when it wholly disappeared.'

The description continues at some length, the minister finishing by stating that, despite particular enquiries, he has not heard of any motion of the earth anywhere but in his own neighbourhood. (This event took place in 1784.)

The report for the parish of Dron, some five miles north from Perth, has this entry under the title 'singular phenomenon': (XII, 138)

> 'After a long series of rainy weather, the hill [part of the Ochils] about 100 paces from the summit, burst open with a loud explosion like thunder, which was heard at the distance of two miles across the valley. A violent and rapid torrent, mixed with earth and stone and broken rock, issued from the opening, and rushed down with an impetuosity which swept all before it. The inhabitants of some houses which stood immediately below, were preparing to flee for their safety, when happily the torrent deviated into a different tract, and after continuing to flow for 10 or 12 hours, it ceased, without having done any material injury, and has remained quiet ever since.'

The writer for the parish of Bendothy in Perthshire describes a more mysterious sight, for which readers may have their own interpretation: (XII, 78)

> 'One night I observed in the air a long narrow stripe of whitish cloud, one end of which was near me; its position was horizontal. The end next to me, as it advanced, became more red, bent into a curve; then revolved upon itself with a very quick spiral motion, and the appearance of

intense fire; and though it was quite calm where I
stood, the phenomenon was attended with the
sound of a whirlwind, which I would have
perceived it to have been, had it been daylight,
and a cloud of dust to make it visible.'

Intriguing as these natural phenomena undoubtedly are,
it is rather memorable stories of human interest which will
probably mean more to some of us. There are, for example,
descriptions of men (and just occasionally women) of
outstanding gifts and achievements, one of whom is a
humble shepherd from the Dollar area: (IX, 766)

'There is living at present in this parish, in a very
advanced age, a man who was bred up, and lived
merely as a shepherd, and who received only a
common education,; and yet possesses a
valuable library of books containing upwards of
370 volumes. They are upon many different
subjects, as divinity, history, travels, voyages &c,
besides magazines of various kinds, such as the
Scots, the Universal, and the other magazines; a
complete set of the Spectator, Guardian, Tatler,
Rambler &c. They are all of them his own
chusing and purchasing. They are neatly bound,
and lettered on the back.'

An amazing character, given the general extreme poverty
of the times; and what a story, were one to know just how

he managed to acquire such treasure!

The local dominie is singled out for special mention by the writer of the Duplin and Aberdalgy account in Perthshire. Following a eulogy of the teacher's general excellence, the minister describes one of his more unusual gifts: (XI, 162)

> 'It will not be deemed improper to add, that he has acquired without any instructor, the rare talent of communicating knowledge to the deaf and dumb, and of teaching them to speak. A boy of this description, not 12 years of age, who never had another teacher, has made a very great proficiency under him. Already he articulates a great many words pretty distinctly, and his articulation appears to be fast improving. He can read, write, and solve any question in the common rules of arithmetic, as well as most boys his age, who do not labour under his disadvantages.'

Another remarkable teacher is mentioned in the report for Aberdour, Aberdeenshire – not least remarkable in that she was a woman, and aged 'upwards of 90 years of age'. She had taught children to read English and knit stockings, the writer tells us, for upwards of forty years, with great success, and 'still has a few scholars.' (XV, 6)

Some stories are clearly included simply for interest or amusement. A good example is this one from the minister of the parish of Montquhitter in Aberdeenshire, who wrote an outstanding report: (XV, 324)

'Those who have been born in the parish are
fondly attached to their native soil.
'How can I live?', said a poor fellow, not destitute
of genius, who had wandered to Edinburgh in
search of business; 'oh, how can I live, out of the
sight of the bonny parks of Auchry?' To the
bonny parks of Auchry his predominant passion
obliged him to return, and he is now active in
increasing the population by a numerous family.'

Another noteworthy story is included in order to underline changes in sartorial customs, in particular the gradual
demise of the traditional blue bonnet: (Laurencekirk XIV, 169)

'As a specimen of the change that has taken place
within these 20 years with regard to dress, it may
be worth mentioning that about 18 or 19 years
ago, a hatter came from Edinburgh to settle in the
village, and having arrived upon a Saturday, but
seeing only three hats in the church beside his
own, he was discouraged, so that he dropped his
scheme and left the place on Monday.'

Several unusual stories are concerned with acute or.
chronic illnesses. An example of the former comes from
Lochcarron in Wester Ross, from where the minister writes
this rather gruesome description: (XVII, 571)

'In 1791, there was a remarkable herring fishing
in this loch. The people fed entirely on fish. They
were visited by a fever. Their blood was vitiated.

When their blood was let, it had the appearance
when it congealed, of a boiled pudding, or of an
ugly type of jelly. Their breath smelled strongly of
fish. In proportion as they fed on fish, the fever
was more or less severe. Such as lived mostly on
fish and other strong food, suffered dreadful
agony. The poorer people who lived mostly upon
water gruel, suffered very little.'

While it is hoped that the mysterious Lochcarron fever
was not repeated, other strange-sounding maladies were
clearly a common occurrence. A bizarre condition is mentioned in several of the Angus reports, for example, as in this
from Lethnot: (XIII, 373)

'There is a distemper, called by the country
people 'the leaping ague', and by physicians 'St
Vitus Dance', which has prevailed for upwards of
60 years in these parishes, and some of the
neighbouring ones. The patient first complains of
a pain in the head, and in the lower part of the
back; to this succeed convulsive fits, or fits of
dancing, leaping or running at certain periods.
The disease appears to be hereditary in some
families.'

Again, from Tannadice in Angus: (XIII, 650)

'Those affected by this disease, when in a
paroxysm, often leap from the floor to what, in
cottages, are called the baulks, or those beams by

which the rafters are joined together. Sometimes they spring from one to another with the agility of a cat, or whirl round one of them with a motion resembling the fly of a jack. At other times they run with astonishing velocity to some particular place out of doors. . . then drop down quite exhausted.'

No less bizarre are the descriptions, this time from Shetland, of another condition, as in this one from Delting: (XIX, 403)

'Convulsive fits of a very extraordinary kind seem peculiar to this country. The patient is at first seized with something like fainting, and immediately after, utters wild cries and shrieks, the sound of which, at whatever distance, immediately puts all who are subject to the disorder in the same situation. It most commonly attacks them when the church is crowded; and often interrupts the service in this, and many other churches in the country. On a sacramental occasion, 50 or 60 are sometimes carried out of the church, and laid in the churchyard.'

Help was at hand, however, for in a neighbouring parish (Northmaven), the hysterical origin of the phenomenon was addressed in no uncertain terms: (XIX, 469)

'Convulsions were once very common in this

parish, especially during the time of divine service; but are now quite extinct. The cure is attributed to a rough fellow of a Kirk Officer, who tossed a woman in that state, with whom he was often plagued, into a ditch full of water. She was never known to have it afterward, and others dreaded the like treatment.'

The most prevalent diseases of the day – attested in report after report – were 'the rheumatism and sundry fevers'. Of fevers particularly there are numerous reports. That they spread without let or hindrance is certainly no surprise, as the following extract from the report for Clunie in Perthshire makes clear: (XII, 220)

'When a fever comes here, it generally attacks numbers. This is owing in a great measure to the temerity of those who, from friendly intentions, visit the patient; but who, without observing proper caution, rush upon his breath, imbibe the contagion, and communicate it from house to house, and from village to village.'

A similar impression that the general standard of hygiene at the time was abysmal is conveyed by the writer for Saline in Fife; the humorous tone belies the seriousness of the observation: (X, 759)

'There is a practice here which, it were to be wished, was abolished. When anyone is taken ill,

> the neighbours think it their duty immediately to
> frequent the house, and even crowd the room
> where the patient lies. On these occasions they
> are all physicians. They feel the pulse, shake their
> heads, and have an unlucky turn to foreboding
> the worst. I have known a man given up by his
> neighbours, who in three or four days after, has
> been working in the stone quarry; and several
> persons who are still alive, in very good health to
> this day and likely to see others carried to their
> graves, who had long ago pronounced their
> doom.'

Considering the general ignorance of hygiene which such extracts demonstrate, it comes as something of a surprise to find a very clear exception in the account for Banff. (But this is part of the fascination of the Old Statistical Account; whatever generalisation one may be tempted to make, it is always possible to unearth a different view!) The Banff minister is in fact emphasising the advice left behind by a previous incumbent: (XVI, 43)

> 'Mr Skene recommends great attention to
> cleanliness, washing the sick person's room with
> soap and water, and upon recovery that his
> apartment should be white-washed with lime,
> and the windows open every day.'

If only such advice had been followed! And yet, given the type of houses, and the scarcity of water and of every kind of convenience, the situation is easy to understand.

Many of the ministers' stories are poignant in the extreme, most of all when they are writing about smallpox. The periodic visitations of this scourge carried off large numbers of people, especially children; in some cases, whole families of children died. It is easy to skim over lists of statistics of the time without stopping to think of the human reality; a single one, however, is sufficient to highlight the kind of tragedies which faced our ancestors from time to time. From the parish of Tarbat in Easter Ross comes this sad entry: (XVII, 645)

> 'The small-pox is the disease which has proved
> most fatal to the rising generation. Its effects were
> particularly calamitous in 1756, when it carried
> off 75 children. In 1768 it cut off 46, and 38 in
> the month of October last (1791). Some families
> at those different times lost their whole children.
> Inoculation when tried failed in only one
> instance, and there are families in this place, in
> which there was not an instance of recovery until
> this method was taken; notwithstanding which,
> the people still retain a strong prejudice against it,
> and seem deaf to all arguments used to shew its
> usefulness and expediency, as a means of which
> Providence has blessed for saving thousands of
> lives.'

Small wonder then that many of the ministers write with passion, raging at the needless waste of so many young lives – as in this excerpt from the report for Kirkmabreck in Galloway: (V, 229)

> 'General as the practice of inoculation has become, yet there are many of these little innocents that fall victim to the inattention, stupidity, and superstition of their parents, who are so wedded to the ancient prejudices, that rather than part with them, they will consign over half a dozen fine children to the ravages of this disorder, or, perhaps, to the gloomy mansions of the tomb.'

All was not gloom, however, for in some places the parents themselves had learned how to inoculate their children; ministers were sometimes brave enough to inoculate their own offspring as examples; most remarkable of all, here and there ordinary working men had somehow become true 'specialists'.

One exceptional story comes from the parish of Mid & South Yell in Shetland. Let the minister describe this particular specialist: (XIX, 542)

> 'Inoculation is successfully practised, even by the common people, but in particular by a person whose name is John Williamson, who, from his various attainments, is called 'Johnny Notions' among his neighbours. Unassisted by education, and unfettered by the rules of art, he stands unrivalled in his business. Several thousands have been inoculated by him, and he has not lost

a single patient. He uses only the best matter, and
keeps it a long time before he puts it to use –
sometimes seven or eight years. And in order to
lessen its virulence he first dries it in peat smoke,
and then puts it under ground covered with
camphor. The only plaister he ever uses for
healing the wound is a bit of cabbage leaf.'

The minister later adds that Johnny had a variety of other
occupations, being a tailor, a joiner, a clock and watch maker,
a blacksmith and a physician!

One disease which caused a great deal of suffering was
scurvy, which is mentioned again and again in the reports;
indeed it is of interest to try to determine from the various
comments whether any knowledge existed as to its true
cause. And, predictably perhaps, the answer is mixed, some
linking the disease clearly to lack of vegetables (fruit, apart
from wild berries, being almost unknown), while others
blame a variety of factors, as here in the report for Forbes &
Kearn, Aberdeenshire: (XV, 139)

'Of all the diseases that prevail here, the scurvy is
the most epidemical, and may justly be called the
bane and scourge of human nature. This
distemper may primarily be contracted from
various causes – like indolent habits,
unwholesome food, impure air, the want of
attention to cleanliness, a sedentary life etc.'

The concept of a disease being actually caused by a

deficiency was not to come until much later.

Many of the stories of good health and especially longevity come as light relief after the sombre descriptions of common diseases. In answering Sir John's question: 'Are there any instances of long lives well authenticated?' it almost seems as if neighbouring ministers are vying with each other to prove the outstanding hardihood of their parishioners. Some descriptions are humorous – whether or not intentionally – as this one from the parish of Halkirk in Caithness: (XVIII, 64)

> 'There is a man in my near neighbourhood, on
> the borders of 80 years, who can number
> upwards of 120 persons of his own progeny,
> besides those who died. The number is still
> increasing by his children, grandchildren, great
> grandchildren etc., and what is of particular
> remark, he is still healthy and vigorous, and is as
> able to add to the number by his own personal
> exertions, as he was several years ago; so that if
> he is spared but a few years, I have no doubt but
> he may see the number doubled.'

Another amusing anecdote in a similar vein comes from Parton in the Borders: (V, 298)

> 'A few years ago, a man died above 90, who,
> about eight months before his death, got a
> complete set of new teeth, which he employed
> till near his last breath to excellent purpose. He

was four times married, had children by all his
wives, and at the baptism of his last child, which
happened not a year before his death, with an air
of complacency expressed his thankfulness to his
Maker for having 'at last sent him the 'cled score'
[the twenty-first].'

Another noteworthy comment comes from the island of
Tiree: (XX, 266)

'A country man, who died last year, about
5ft 10ins high, was employed by the Laird of Coll
as post to Glasgow or Edinburgh. His ordinary
burden thence to Coll was 16 stone. Being once
stopped at a toll near Dumbarton, he humorously
asked whether he should pay for the burden, and
upon being answered in the negative, carried his
horse in his arms past the toll.'

Although it is well known that the horses of the day were
habitually skinny and ill-fed in comparison with ours today,
this still ranks as no mean feat!

One story which is nothing if not somewhat enigmatic
concerns one of the healing wells to which the folk of the
day attached great importance. This comes from the report
for Kirkconnel: (IV, 277)

'An Englishman, suffering from florid scurvy, who
had been dismissed from Carlisle Infirmary as
incurable, came to take the waters at Kirkconnel.
To say nothing of other effects of the scorbutic

> habit he laboured under, he was quite emaciated,
> bowed down, feeble and dispirited. But after the
> regular use of the water, he gradually recovered,
> till in about eight weeks he became quite well,
> and went away stout, and lively, and joyous,
> because of his unexpected and remarkable
> recovery.'

Remarkable indeed. . . unless perhaps he had been eating rosehips at the same time?

Another enigma emerges from two separate parish accounts. What, one wonders, is the magic ingredient in soil which apparently produces good crops without any kind of manure? Here is the first – from Kilmorack near Beauly: (XVII, 170)

> 'New experiments are frequently made in the
> culture of potatoes, and many of them have
> succeeded beyond expectation. The present
> incumbent has had 11 successive crops from one
> field without a particle of manure, and all, except
> the last, equally good. He has now the satisfaction
> to see many of his parishioners following his
> example. The potatoes thus raised are, in number
> and size, at least equal and in quality far superior,
> to those laid down with the richest manure.'

An equally enigmatic situation seems to have prevailed in Dalmeny in the Lothians, where a phenomenon known as 'perpetual soil' is described: (II, 727)

'In this parish are a few spots of what is called 'perpetual soil', exceedingly fertile, and which have had no dung, it is said, in the memory of man. Part of the minister's garden is of this kind, which has long been known to produce great crops, and of late, surprising ones of potatoes have been reared. For experiment's sake, potatoes were lately planted on a portion of it, six years running, and the last crop was as good as the first. Dung was applied one year, but the plants ran to stalks and leaves; the roots were numerous, but very small.'

Still on the subject of agriculture, an intriguing breeding experiment seems well worth a mention. It comes from the report from Colvend and Southwick in the Borders: (V, 89)

'About six or seven years ago a gentleman of the parish, then master of a vessel in the Baltic trade, purchased from some Laplanders a Lapland ram with four horns, of about the size and weight of the common black-faced sheep of this country; but his great excellence was his fleece, which was very abundant, and remarkably fine and silky. He brought him home to this country, with which he seemed to agree very well. He was observed to delight much in cropping the heather, and to prefer it to any other plant the climate produced. He lived 18 months here, and experienced all our variety of season. He propagated with ewe of this country.'

The tale ends sadly:

'Both he and his offspring were killed by some
other animal, by which means the breed was
unfortunately lost.'

One entry from Peterculter near Aberdeen is nothing if
not original, being set out by the writer in a form unhappily
reminiscent of school problems in arithmetic: (XIV, 668)

'Tenants who live on the banks of a burn
sometimes build a fish-garth. They catch some
trout and some pike, but eels in great
abundance.'

The minister then proceeds with his mathematical
calculation, the exact purpose of which is not clear:

'Some assert that two eels at least pass in one
second; say three in two seconds, or 90 in a
minute; or 37,800 in an hour, which being
doubled for both sides of the river, makes 75,500
in an hour, or 1,814,400 in a natural day.'

One comment which is truly remarkable for its prophetic
vision, of two canals which are of great importance today,
comes from the report for Gigha and Cara: (XX, 445)

'By a canal through the isthmus at Crinan, the
navigation between the Western Isles and Clyde
would be rendered safe, easy and expeditious, at

all seasons of the year. By another canal between
Inverness and Fort William, a direct
communication would be opened from the west
to the east coast of Scotland, which would be not
only of infinite mutual advantage to both these
districts of the kingdom, but to the commercial
interests of England and Ireland.'

It may be of some interest to record here a few of the
more memorable entries to Sir John's question about manufactures: in Dysart, Fife, '43 smiths make six million nails
annually' – these being 'fashioned from old iron imported
from Holland'. (X, 335) In the Perthshire village of Doune,
surprisingly, the making of pistols is described thus: (XII,
534)

'The only remains of any of the ancient branches
of trade is the making of Highland pistols. . . In
the year 1646, the famous tradesman Thomas
Caddell brought his work to so high degree of
perfection that no pistols made in Britain
excelled, or perhaps equalled, those of his
making, either for sureness, strength, or beauty.'

The making of shoes – no fewer than 24,000 pairs
annually – kept around 100 persons busy in Linlithgow (II,
760), while from Easdale in Argyll the slate quarries produced
some five million slates each year, exported by ship 'whether
bound for the Baltic, Ireland, Leith, or London.' (XX, 62)

A suitable ending to this chapter of unusual and memorable extracts is provided by the minister of Lochcarron in Wester Ross, who whimsically concludes his account in verse: (XVII, 577)

> 'This same statistical account
> Is sent to please Sir John
> And if it is not elegant
> Let critics throw a stone
> We have not fine materials
> And our account is plain
> Our lands and purling streams are good
> But we have too much rain. . .
>
> Sir John, send word, if you are pleased
> With what I here rehearse
> Perhaps 'twere better had I told
> My story all in verse.
> This parson has no horse, nor farm
> No goat, no watch, no wife
> Without an augmentation too
> He leads a happy life.'

Some Interesting Statistics

The following shows a selection of answers to Sir John's questions regarding trades and professions within the parishes. Those illustrated here are from different areas of Scotland.

It is of interest to note not only the remarkable number of trades carried on even in very rural parishes, but also how the list becomes as it were more sophisticated in the more prosperous towns and also, for example, in Inveresk near the capital. A study of the lists tells one a great deal about the country in the late eighteenth century.

Example 1

Stromness, Orkney:

(Sandwick & Stromness XIX, 238)

Male servants	–	Joiners	8
Female servants	118	Masons	13
Seamen	60	Coopers	7
Ship carpenters	18	Blacksmiths	15
Shopkeepers	25	Flaxdressers	3
Weavers	15	Day-labourers	22
Tailors	11	Writers	2
Shoemakers	13	Custom house surveyors	2
		Tide waiters	3
		Boatmen	6
		Surgeons	1
		Clergymen	1

Example 2
Kirriemuir in Angus (XIII, 367)

Population 4,358
Predominantly a weaving town

Clergymen	2
Merchants	30
Surgeons	2
Schoolmasters	7
Farmers	78
Innkeepers	14
Smiths	12
Masons	28
Carpenters	50
Weavers	576
Shoemakers	56
Tailors	39
Butchers	4
Millers	25
Gardeners	9
Male servants	–
Female servants	96
Male farm servants	290
Female farm servants (occasional)	251
Flaxdressers	18
Day labourers	47

'No town in the country has a better weekly market; in none of its size is more trade carried on.'

Example 3
Cupar, Fife (X, 231):

Attorneys or writers	12
Clerks to ditto	20
Medical practitioners	5
Clergymen	3
School-masters	3
Private teachers	4
Mantua-makers	10
Milliners	6
House painters	3
Stationers	2
Bakers & servants	19
Butchers & ditto	16
Brewers	5
Tailors	29
Dyers	5
Masons	21
Wrights	48
Smiths	24
Glovers	5
Hatters	2
Barbers	7
Saddlers	5
Candle-makers	2
Linen merchants	6
Shop-keepers	31
Midwives	4
Watch-makers	3
Excise officers	3
Carriers	4

Messengers 3

Footmen 20

With its milliners, mantua-makers, glovers, and watch-makers, not to mention numerous bakers – scarce indeed in Scotland at the time – Cupar certainly appears to have been a prosperous town!

Example 4

Newton-upon-Ayr, Ayrshire (VI, 498), population 1689

Weavers	101
Wrights	25
Carpenters	24
Shoemakers	10
Sailors	5
Shipmasters	14
Smiths	8
Stocking weavers	7
Coopers	2
Bakers	4
Salmon fishers	22
White fishers	26
Herring fishers	12
Colliers	24
Day labourers	57
Clothiers or dyers	3
Travelling chapmen	11

(mostly Irish)

Ropemakers	10
Braziers, tinkers, horners	5
Masons	7
Land labourers	5
Carriers	9
Female servants	59
Male servants	3
School masters	3
Customs officers	3
Excise officers	2
Grocers	6
Carters	2
Tanners	2
Curriers	3
Skinners	4
Clock makers	2
Toll-gatherers	2
Butcher	1
Barber	1
Gardener	1
Miller	1
Heelmaker	1
Maltman	1
Gun-smith	1
Messenger-at-arms	1
Musician	1
Drummer	1

Example 5, Inveresk

(outskirts of Edinburgh)
(II, 301) Population 5392

Wrights and smiths	70
Tailors	30
Shoemakers	96
Bakers	44
Gardeners	16
Weavers	140
Fleshers	50
Masons	40
Grocers	10
Fishermen	49
Fish-wives	90
Salt-wives	50
Wine-merchants	40
Milliners	2
Mantua-makers	10
Hairdressers	6
Perfumers	2
Carters	63

Note the non-essential trades, such as perfumers, hairdressers, mantua-makers, indicating a more affluent population.

Diseases

A few of the ministers furnished a list of the causes of death in their parishes. Here are three, each from different areas of Scotland:

HIGHLAND AREA
Alvie, Inverness-shire (XVII, 6)
'Died between 1 February 1792 & 1 February 1793':

Fevers	6
Consumption	3
Sudden death	2
Chincough [whooping cough]	1
Inward inflammation	1
Old age	1
Hives	1
Scurvy	1

CENTRAL AREA
Campsie, Stirlingshire (IX, 250)
'Of the last three years of burials, the diseases stand thus':

Fevers	8
Small-pox	15
Consumptions	26
Palsy	2

Asthma	1
Chincough	6
Bowel-hive	1
Measles	6
Child-bed	1
Stillborn	1
Mortification	1
Old age	26

NORTH-EAST AREA

Benholme, Kincardineshire (XIV, 40) (period not stated):

Fevers	60
Rush fevers	5
Consumption	21
Decay	77
Dropsy	29
Palsy	11
Small-pox	43
Chincough	8
Child-bed	7
Casualties	24
Asthma	8
Old age	36

Casualties:

Drowned	6
Suffocated	2
Killed in battle	1
Fell from horse	1
Mad dog's bite	1
Fell into fire	1

Budget

Here is the detailed budget of a day-labourer, his wife and family. Several are included in the accounts, but they are so similar that only one need be detailed here.

Auchterderran, Fife (X, 46): 'Annual earnings of a day-labourer, wife, and three children, deduction four weeks' earnings of the man on account of holidays, bad health, attendance at funerals &c, and excessive bad weather; and four weeks' earnings of the woman, on account of holidays, bad health, and lying-in.

To 48 weeks' labour of a man at 1s. a day	£14/8/0
To 48 weeks' labour of a woman, in spinning, besides taking care of her house and children	£3/12/0
To the earnings of three children at the age of six, seven and eight years	0/0/0
Total	£18/0/0

ANNUAL EXPENSES

By 2 pecks oatmeal a week,
at 1$\frac{1}{2}$d. per week £4/19/8
By 2 pecks barley or pease
meal a week at 7$\frac{1}{2}$d. £3/5/0
By 6 bolls potatoes,
at 5s. the boll £1/10/0
By barley for kail,
at 3lb a week £0/16/3
By a kail-yard, and a
wretched house £0/13/0
By milk,
at 4d. a week £0/17/4
By salt, cheese/butter £0/12/6
By soap
for washing clothes £0/2/6
By coals in a year,
and carriage £1/0/0
By shoes
to the whole family £1/0/0
By body clothes
to the man £1/10/0
By ditto to the woman
and children £1/5/0
By worsted thread
for mendings £0/7/0
Total £17/18/3

The writer points out that this family 'manages' because of the small number of children, and the woman's ability to work. 'The greatest evils of their situation', he adds, 'arise from the lowness of their diet, and the wretchedness of their lodging, which is cold, dark, and dirty.'

This family has remained solvent, by a short head. Sadly many others, just as frugal, did not. The minister offering a similar budget for a family in Moulin Perthshire adds this comment:

'Although there appears to be a deficiency of earnings, after the charges have been estimated in the most frugal and even scanty manner, and no allowance made for casual expenses, it is certain that in this country, people who seem to have no livelihood but the fruits of their daily labour, do, by some means or another, bring up families, and even give their children such education as the nearest school affords.' (XII, 757)

Life Expectancy

Some statistics showing longevity in the various regions:

HIGHLANDS:
Avoch, Ross-shire (XVII, 310)
Population 2,318

Age 50-60	116
Age 60-70	5
Age 70-80	30
Age 80-90	9

WESTERN ISLES:
Kilfinichen & Kilviceuen
(Mull) (XX, 300)
Population 323

Age 50-60	23
Age 60-70	65
Age 80	2
Age 85	2
Age 100+	1

CENTRAL:
Coupar, Angus (XI, 92)
Population 2,076

Age 50-60	23
Age 60-70	109
Age 70-80	21
Age 80-90	9

SOUTHWEST:
Dundonald, Ayrshire (VI, 174)
Population 1,317

Age 50-60	82
Age 60-70	43
Age 70-80	26
Age 80-90	3
Age 90-100	1

APPENDIX II

The following pages are a transcription of the original questionnaire sent out to all the parishes in Scotland.

Copy of the QUERIES drawn up for the purpose of elucidating the Natural History and Political State of Scotland, which were enclosed in the preceding letter.
QUESTIONS reflecting the GEOGRAPHY
and NATURAL HISTORY of the PARISH.
1. What is the ancient and modern name of the Parish?
2. What is the origin and etymology of the name?
3. In what county is it situated?
4. In what presbytery and synod?
5. What is the extent and form of the parish?
6. What its length and breadth?
7. By what parishes is it bounded?
8. What is the general appearance of the country? Is it flat or hilly, rocky or mountainous?
9. What is the nature of the soil? Is it fertile or barren, deep or shallow?
10. What is the nature of the air? Is it moist or dry, unhealthy or otherwise?
11. What are the most prevalent distempers? And to what circumstances are they to be attributed?
12. Are there any mineral springs? And in what diseases are they serviceable?
13. Are there any considerable lakes or rivers in the parish?
14. What species of fish do they produce? In what quantities? What prices do they fetch on the spot? And in what seasons are they in the greatest perfection?
15. Are the rivers navigable? Or might they be rendered useful in navigation?
16. Are there any navigable canals in the parish?
17. What is the extent of sea coast?
18. Is the shore flat, sandy, high or rocky?
19. What sorts of fish are caught on the coast? In what quantity? At what prices sold? When most in season? How taken? And to what markets sent?
20. What other sea animals, plants, sponges, corals, shells etc are found on or near the coast?

21. Are there any remarkable sea weeds used for manuring land, or curious on any other account?
22. Is there any kelp? And what quantity, at an average, is annually made?
23. What are the courses of the tides on the shore or at sea? And are there any rocks, currents, etc worthy of notice?
24. Are there any lighthouses, beacons, or land-marks? Or could any be erected that would be of service?
25. What are the names of the principal creeks, bays, harbours, headlands, sands or islands, near the coast?
26. Have there been any battles or sea fights near the coast? And when did any remarkable wrecks or accidents happen, which can give light to any historical fact?
27. Are there any remarkable mountains? And what are their heights?
28. Are the hills covered with heath, green, or rocky?
29. Are there any volcanic appearances in the parish?
30. Are there any figured stones, or any having the impression of plants or fibres upon them?
31. Are there any fossil marine bodies such as shells, corals, etc or any petrified part of animals? or any petrifying springs or waters?
32. Are there any marble, moor-stone, free stone, slate or other stones? How are they got at, and what use is made of them?
33. Are there any mines, particularly coal-mines? What are they? To whom do they belong? And what do they produce?
34. Is any part of the parish subject to inundations or land-floods? When did any remarkable event of that nature happen?
35. Hath there been any remarkable mischief done by thunder and lightning, water-spouts or whirlwinds?
36. Are there any remarkable echoes?
37. Have any remarkable phenomena been observed in the air?
38. Are there any remarkable caves or grottos, natural or artificial?
39. What quadrupeds and birds are there in the parish? What migratory birds? and what times do they appear and disappear?
40. Is the parish remarkable for breeding any species of cattle, sheep, horses, hogs, or goats, of peculiar quality, size, or value?

II QUESTIONS reflecting the POPULATION of the PARISH?
41. What was the ancient state of the population of the parish, so far as it can be traced?
42. What is now the amount of its population?
43. What may be the number of males?
44. What of females;
45. How many reside in towns?
46. _____villages?
47. _____the country?
48. What is the annual average of births?

49. _____deaths?*
50. _____marriages?
51. _____souls under 10 years of age?
52. _____from 10 to 20?
53. _____20 to 50?
54. _____50 to 70
55. _____70-100?
56. _____Above 100?
57. Are there any instances of long lives well authenticated?
58. What may be the number of farmers and their families?
59. _____manufacturers?
60. _____handycraftsmen?
61. _____apprenctices?
62. _____seamen?
63. _____fishermen?
64. _____ferrymen?
65. _____miners?
66. _____household servants, male and female?
67. _____labouring servants, male and female?
68. _____students at colleges and universities?
69. _____merchants, citizens or tradesmen?
70. _____artists?
71. _____Jews?
72. _____negroes?
73. _____gipsies?
74. _____foreigners
75. _____persons born in England, Ireland, or the British colonies?
76. What may be the number of persons born in other districts or parishes?
77. What may be the number of the nobility and their families?
78. _____gentry?
79. _____clergy?

---

* It is of peculiar importance to have the questions 48 and 49 distinctly answered; for it is generally understood, at least on the Continent, that the population of any district or country, may be known with sufficient accuracy, by multiplying the number of births by 26, or the number of deaths by 36. In Scotland, on the other hand, Mr Wilkie, minister of Cults, supposes, that the number either or births and burials, if they are equal, should be multiplied by the expectation of an infant's life, adapted to the particular district, in order to ascertain its population. See Statistical Account, vol. II. p. 415. It appears, from Mr Wilkie's calculations, that the expectation of a life in Scotland, is much greater than in England, or on the Continent.

80. _____lawyers and writers or attorneys?
81. _____physicians, surgeons, and apothecaries?
82. _____the established church?
83. _____seceders?
84. _____episcopalians?
85. _____Roman Catholics?
86. Is the population of the parish materially different from what it was 5, 10, or 25 years ago? And to what causes is the alteration attributed?
87. What is the proportion between the annual births and the whole population?
88. What is the proportion between the annual marriages and the whole population?
89. What is the proportion between the annual deaths and the whole population?
90. What is the proportion between the bachelors and the married men, widowers included?
91. How many children does each marriage at an average produce?
92. What may be the causes of depopulation?
93. Are there any destructive epidemical distempers?
94. Have any died from want?
95. Have any murders or suicide been committed?
96. Have many emigrated from the parish?
97. Have any been banished from it?
98. Have any been obliged to leave the parish for want of employment?
99. Are there any uninhabited houses?
100. What may be the number of uninhabited houses, and the number of persons at an average to each inhabited house?

III QUESTIONS reflecting the PRODUCTIONS of the PARISH
101. What kinds of vegetables, plants, and trees, does the parish produce?
102. What kind of animals?
103. What at an average is supposed to be the number of cattle, sheep, horses, hogs, and goats, in the district?
104. Is there any map of the parish? and has the number of acres in it been ascertained?
105. How many acres at an average may be employed in raising corn, roots, etc?
106. What number of acres to each sort respectively, as wheat, barley, rye, oats, potatoes, turnip, cabbage, etc?
107. Does the parish supply itself with provisions?
108. Does it in general export or import articles of provision?
109. How many acres are employed in raising hemp or flax?
110. How many in sown or artificial grasses?
111. How many in pasture?
112. When do they in general sow and reap their different crops?

113. What quantity of ground may lie waste or in common?
114. What in woods, forests, marshes, lakes, and rivers?
115. Is there any chalk, marl, fullers earth, potters earth, ochre, etc?
116. Are there any bitumen, naptha, or other substances of that nature found in the soil?

IV MISCELLANEOUS QUESTIONS
117. Has the parish any peculiar advantages or disadvantages?
118. What language is principally spoken in it?
119. From what language do the names of places in the parish seem to be derived?
120. What are the most remarkable instances of such derivations?
121. What may the land rent of the parish be?
122. What the rent of the houses, fishings, etc?
123. What is the value of the living, including the glebe? and who is the patron?
124. Who is now minister of the parish?
125. How long has be been settled in it?
126. What are the names of his predecessors as far back as they can now be traced, and the time they respectively held that office?
127. Is the minister married, a widower, or single?
128. If with a family, how many sons, and how many daughters?
129. When were the church and manse built or repaired?
130. What is the number of heritors, or possessors of landed property in the parish?
131. How many of them reside in it?
132. What is the number of the poor in the parish receiving alms?
133. What is the annual amount of the contributions for their relief, and the produce of alms, legacies, or of any other fund destined for that purpose?
134. What are the recent or ancient prices of provisions, beef, veal, mutton, lamb, pork, pigs, geese, ducks, chickens, rabbits, butter, cheese, wheat, barley, oats, etc?
135. What is generally a day's wages for labourers in husbandry, and other work? and what per day for carpenters, bricklayers, masons, tailors, etc?
136. What is the fuel commonly made use of? Is it coal, wood, heath, peat, furze, or whins? What are the prices paid on the spot; and whence is the fuel procured?
137. What, at an average, may be the expense of a common labourer, when married? and is the wages he receives sufficient to enable him to bring up a family?
138. What are the usual wages of male and female servants in the different branches of husbandry?

139. What are the wages of domestic servants?
140. How many ploughs are there in the parish? and of what kinds?
141. How many carts and wagons?
142. How many carriages; and what sorts?
143. Are there any villages in the parish? and how are they situated?
144. Are there any crosses or obelisks erected in the parish?
145. Are there any remains or ruins of monasteries or religious houses?
146. Are there any Roman, Saxon, Danish, or Pictish castles, camps, altars, roads, forts. Or other remains of antiquity? and what traditions or historical accounts are there of them?
147. Have there been any medals, coins, arms, or other pieces of antiquity dug up in the parish? When were they found? And in whose custody are they now?
148. Are there any barrow, or tumuli? Have they been opened? and what has been found therein?
149. Have there been any remarkable battles fought in the parish? On what spot? At what time? By whom? And what traditions are there respecting the fame?
150. Has the parish either given birth or burial to any man eminent for learning, or distinguished for any other valuable qualification?
151. Are the people of the country remarkable for strength, size, complexion, or any other personal or mental qualities?
152. What is the general size of the people?
153. What is the greatest height which any individual in the parish has attained, properly authenticated?
154. Are the people disposed to industry? What manufactures are carried on in the parish? And what number of hands are employed therein?
155. Are the people fond of a sea-faring life? What is the number of boats and of larger vessels belonging to the parish? And what number of seamen have entered into the navy during any preceding war?
156. Are the people fond of a military life? Do many enlist in the army? And principally in what corps?
157. Are the people economical, or expensive and luxurious for their circumstances? Is property, particularly in land, often changing? And at what prices is it in general sold?
158. Are the people disposed to humane and generous actions; to protect and relieve the shipwrecked, etc? and are there any events which have happened in the parish, which do honour to human nature?
159. Do the people, on the whole, enjoy, in a reasonable degree, the comforts and advantages of society? And are they contented with their situation and circumstances?
160. Are there any means by which their condition could be ameliorated?

ADDENDA

1. What is the state of the roads and bridges in the parish? How were they originally made? How are they kept in repair? Is the statute labour exacted in kind, or commuted? Are there any turnpipkes? and what is the general opinion of the advantages of turnpike roads?
2. What is in general the rent of the best arable and the best pasture or meadow grounds, per acre? What the rent of inferior?
3. What in general is the size and the average rent of the farms in the parish? And is the number of farms increasing or diminishing?
4. Is the parish in general enclosed, or unenclosed? And are the people convinced of the advantages of enclosures?
5. What was the situation of the parish anno 1782 and 1783? Please state any curious or important circumstances connected with that era, or with any other season of scarcity.
6. Are there any curious or important facts tending to prove any great alteration in the manners, customs, dress, style of living, etc. of the inhabitants of the parish, now, and 20 or 50 years ago?

N.B. If you reside in a town or city, please give an account of the history and antiquities of the place; of its buildings, age, walls, sieges, charters, privileges, immunities, gates, streets, markets, fairs; the number of churches, wards, guilds, companies, fraternities, clubs, etc.: How the town is governed: if it is represented in parliament, to whom does the right of election belong, and what the number of electors? together with a comparison between its ancient and modern state, in regard to population, commerce, shipping, fisheries, manufactures, more particularly at the following periods, about the time of the Union, since the year 1745, and at present.